"THIS BO PEEP AIN'T NO FAIRY TALE!!"

"THIS BO PEEP AIN'T NO FAIRY TALE!!"

A Book by Murray M. Silver

2/20/2002

To: Hon. Linda Wittish:

Thank You!

Best Wishes for Your continued success!

Murray M. Silver

ISBN: 0-75960-436-3

Front cover photograph by Murray M. Silver, taken in front of
"Bo Peep's" on August 29, 1942.

This book is printed on acid free paper.

"A Psalm of Life" (1834) by Henry Wadsworth Longfellow,
2/27/1807 – 3/24/1882.

1stBooks – rev. 01/02/01

ACKNOWLEDGEMENTS

Although hundreds of people asked: "Why don't you write a Book about your Dad?" It took a long time to separate the wheat from the chaff, and set aside necessary time. Several people helped me in the writing of this memoir. Six, I would particularly like to cite are, my Mother, Catherine Mendel Silver, whose love and devotion was constant, even during the bad times; my Wife, Barbara Kahn Silver, a source of love, patience and understanding provided invaluable aid; my two Sons, Murray M. Silver, Jr., and Eric Carl Silver, whose unfailing love, loyalty, devotion and friendship made me a good Father and a better man; Hon. S. Sam Caldwell, former Commissioner of Labor of Georgia, who extended the hand of freindship, and, Rev. Dr. Martin Luther "Daddy" King, who was always "there" with kind words of encouragement, guidance, and constant reminder: "Counsellor, the Lord ain't done with you "YET!"

I am their humble servant.

INTRODUCTION

I am a novice at writing memoirs. It is probably one of the most difficult projects a person can undertake, but it does afford an opportunity to sum up a few of the years and hopefully provide insights to an incredibly complex man, my Father.

The subject has complete control over the book's contents. It is written in truth, the whole truth and nothing but the truth. I can vouch for the accuracy of the descriptions of people and events, both from my own memory and the memories of all those to whom I talked. I conducted several interviews during my research. The conversations from them were all recorded and the quotes I have used accurately reflect what was said.

Many of the leading players are gone. Almost all of whom I miss because they were nice to me and helped me. Others, were not kind, and I find myself wishing they would still be alive, so that I could strut my stuff in front of them.

This book is respectfully dedicated to my Father, who loved his Family so completely, and, whose departure was all too soon; a victim of bad luck; and, to all acquaintances who helped me along the way.

I love him, and you all!

CHAPTER ONE

Once upon a time, in the land of good and evil, there lived a little man who became a legend in his own time.

Now, everybody knows the children's nursery rhyme, "Little Bo Peep." But, children, you ain't heard nothing yet!

"Little Bo Peep lost his sheep, and don't know where to find them; leave them alone, and they will come home, wagging their tails behind them."

Prepare now for a remarkable journey from rags to riches, with all the ups and downs one man could face in a life time. A very special journey filled with those events that alter and illuminate our lives, and, hey, you were there!

It all began in the year 1929 when WOLFE W. SILVER opened a small lunch kitchen and billiard parlor. These were the very lean years in America, the year of the great stock market crash that knocked Wall Street and America for a loop. Depression, not only financial and spiritual but also mental pervaded throughout the country.

This is a true story written by one who was present during the years from 1929 through 1963. In some instances the names of persons have been changed to protect their "innocence" and identity. Everything and everybody is factual and incredibly amazing, filled with humor and pathos, a story about Savannah, Georgia, U. S. A., and some of its inhabitants.

Wolfe Silver was born in London, England on October 25, 1899. His father Max was of German-Jewish heritage; his Mother Jennie, English-Jewish heritage, settled in Savannah shortly thereafter. He attended a public school for the first three grades, then quit to go to work shining shoes, to help his family of three sons, two daughters, mother and father. They lived near the Savannah River at the intersection of Williamson Street and West Broad in a small three bedroom, one bath, stucco-brick, two story building. The origin of the family name "Silver" is in doubt, as he frequently stated, "It was the first name we saw on a sign, when we arrived in America." With just a little schooling, he could read and write German, at the same time, he was fluent in "Yiddish," which he learned from his Mother and Father.

As a child, he never knew what it was like to have "new clothes," always the recipient of "hand-me-downs," or second hand garments. Shoes came from "used shoes on West Broad Street." "I cannot remember when I got my first new clothes or shoes; I believe I was twelve or thirteen."

Raised in an Orthodox Jewish home environment, attended B. B. Jacob Synagogue, walked to services Saturday mornings with sisters Annie and Esther. A "kosher" kitchen was steadfastly adhered to and rules complied with by his Mother, the cement that kept the family close. In the early years Jews were kept together not only by internal cohesion but also by external exclusion. Proud of being a Jew, he wore it as a badge of courage, eventually insisting that his four children be raised as "good Jews."

Housing was clean but crowded, leading to his fervent desire to "get out and earn money!" He possessed an absolute disdain and indeed hatred for laziness. From his background, it is easy to understand his drive and desire to improve himself and family. After all, he heard that, "In America the streets are paved with gold." His mission, to find those streets. One thing was certain, they weren't named River or Williamson Streets.

The parents owned and operated a small grocery-type store at the corner of West Broad and River Street, approximately one hundred yards from their residence. They sold bread, cookies, candy, chewing gum, cigarettes, kosher barrel pickles and soft drinks. They scarcely earned enough to survive.

"Wolfie" as he was affectionately called did whatever he could to make money. Ran errands, shined shoes, sold newspapers and anything else he could sell.

Early in 1929, at the ripe age of 29, he had amassed funds to open a small "pool room" and lunch counter, that became a Savannah landmark, known around the world, and named it "BO PEEP'S," 19 East Congress Street, "The Finest in the South!"

How did his nickname "BO PEEP" originate? Back during the days of prohibition when a fellow could not buy a drink of whiskey or liquor legally, that the "wise guys" determined that money could be made buying "moonshine" or non-tax paid liquor and deliver it to customers in "dry counties" all across the eastern part of the U. S. of A. He was contacted by Al Capone, and associates, to pick up liquor in New Orleans, La., and transport it back to Georgia, and/or Chicago, Ill. On his second trip he was stopped by law enforcement authorities in Louisiana, detained, and load of liquor declared illegal contraband, seized, three vehicles confiscated.

Perhaps we should recall those events that preceded the confiscation. On or about January 15, 1928, Wolfe was ready to earn money. Tired of "just getting by," he listened attentively to a "feeler," as to whether or not there was any interest in transporting some liquor, or as some called it, "white lightening," "moon shine," or kick-a-poo juice," from New Orleans, Louisiana to Chicago, Illinois, for none other than Al "Scarface" Capone? Indicating a slight interest, the complete details were inquired into, and provided.

After careful consideration, for all of about "three shakes of a fat dog's tail," he consented, conditioned upon the fact that a trial run be made determining the risks, conditions and time necessary. After all, there were no super highways or interstates, the best roads were two lanes. An acquaintance named "Moxie" Callahan, a talkative, little, Irish man, was invited to "come along, for the ride, just for company."

The trip went off without a hitch, except that some unpaved roads were utilized in Alabama and Mississippi. Everything, down to the tire pressure was carefully noted. When, where and how long to stop for food and gasoline. Make no mistakes about it, this first trip had to be exactly right. As a bit of curiosity, two Alabama deputy sheriffs were casually interviewed in an effort to determine shifts.

What was this "prohibition crap," all about anyway?

Laws were enacted making it illegal to manufacture and/or distribute alcoholic beverages. Briefly stated, in the Nineteenth Century, "Temperance Movements," in the states urged prohibition, and the Prohibition Party in 1869 made it a national issue. It gained impetus in World War, I, when conservation policies limited liquor output. In 1919, the Eighteenth Amendment to the Constitution of the United States, established prohibition; but enforcement, through the Volstead Act, failed to abolish "Bootlegging," and the wide spread law breaking associated with it.

Local officials, in conjunction with federal revenue agents sought out and prosecuted violators of the ban on alcohol.

In 1933, the Twenty-first Amendment repealed prohibition.

"Well, let's get ready to rumble."

Wolfe owned a 1928 model Packard "Eight," seven passenger, color green, Touring sedan, for which he paid the astronomical price of Four Thousand, Forty Dollars ($4,040.00) new.

"What a beautiful car, and it could really go fast, up to about 75 miles per hour!"

One 1926 model Ford Truck, and one 1927 Chevrolet Truck bearing Georgia license plates were acquired from

5

friends, and neighbors, who knew not what they were to be used. "Don't worry, everything is alright."

Two drivers, Harry Verushki and Peter Loumakis along with two assistant drivers, and "old reliable, Moxie" Callahan were hired to make the "run." Expenses and arrangements were made in advance, as well as "Cash," to purchase the liquor. Chicago made the contact in New Orleans, including a "password," quantity, choice of container. Each vehicle to transport three, fifty gallon kegs on this initial effort.

Routes to travel, vehicles remain in line, not less than one hundred feet apart; expected "hot spots or traps," delineated on road maps and underlined in red. The trio agreed to proceed non-stop, except for food, gas and "potty time." Leave Savannah early evening on Friday, drive straight through to New Orleans, using the exact route of the trial run; traveling south westerly direction to Waycross, Valdosta and Thomasville, Georgia; south to Tallahassee and Pensacola, Florida; Mobile, Alabama; west to Pascagoula, and Biloxi, Mississippi; the home stretch to Hammond, Louisiana; finally, to New Orleans, the "land of Cajun Queens and sleepy dreams," A distance over one thousand miles. The last fifty of which they were to pick up an "escort," to direct them to the warehouse on Bourbon Street, in the world famous French Quarter "downtown New Orleans."

This was the first visit to "sin city," for the six, they had "Hot Buttered Rum" drink at *Preservation Hall*, dinner at the landmark, *"Antoine's Restaurant."* Incredible, memorable, occasions.

Plans were changed, by the "man in Chicago," the trio was directed to "return to Savannah, place the liquor in safe keeping there, until further notice." "Hot Dog, home again, home again, jiggety-jog!"

Going home was a lot more fun, as the three took turns leading the "convoy." They learned one important detail, tire pressure must be increased to compensate for the additional one thousand, two hundred pounds, and make damn sure the kegs were securely tied to avoid sudden shifting. Rear seats in the "Eight," had been removed providing ample space in the trunk and rear of the automobile. Home is where the heart is. The six were tired but happy fellows.

Now, safely back, the six decided they should keep their exploits "secret." "Let's just take the stuff down to Tybee and hide it on the back river near Merritt Dixon's house. Nobody gonna' go there, this time of year, and ain't no questions to be asked. Paint them kegs with black creosote paint and, who in Hell will know the diffrence?" "Good idea." "Certainly!" Mission accomplished.

Two weeks elapsed before additional contact occurred between the principals. "I will send my boys there to pick the package up, don't worry, the terms of the deal is firm, we will do more and better, next time. Orleans said it all was smooth, and they liked what they saw. Maybe this will be the start of something big, and, if you ever in Chi-town, you got my number, I will see you have a real good time, yes sir!"

What a difference a day makes. Twenty- four little hours.

That night, at home, Wolfe sat quietly in the back room of his two bed room apartment, reflecting upon the events of that week, and three preceding, some what relieved, and, at the same time hopeful. Now he had some "operating money," or, as he was fond of saying, "Money in my kick." "Money in the hand is the sweetest thing in the land."

Anxiously awaiting that next telephone call, actually counting the days, like a child before Christmas. Every time the phone rang, his heart leaped up into his throat. The vigil lasted three more weeks. Then in the late evening he got a call with instructions to, "stand by for news!" "Hooray!"

The phone rang early the following morning, the first bringer of welcome news. Wiping sleep from his eyes, answered in a raspy voice, "Hello!"

"Please get ready now for your trip to New Orleans, and, this time, all the way to Chicago. Arrangements have been made for next Wednesday, the money is right and will be done same as the last time."

Now, the waiting began anew, necessary preparations undertaken, contact the "team," inspect vehicles, plan for a four day journey.

"Ready!"

"Set!"

"Go!"

Three pairs of happy guys met at the foot of the viaduct, dawn the following Wednesday. Early morning stench from the *Union Bag Paper Mill,* was so heavy and thick, "you could cut it with a knife," irritating eyes and nostrils of three men. "Man, it's going to be nice to breathe some clear air for a change," Harry observed; "You would think by now, something could be done to cure this problem."

"Are you kidding, that's the smell of money, and the Bag is deep," Wolfe reminded his pal. "Them folks hire a lot of people, so, I don't see no change any time soon." "Let's go, I'll lead the way, Harry, you follow me and Peter Lou will bring up the rear." "There you go again, talking about Greeks rears!"

It all seemed like Christmas Eve, a very festive and excited six departed on what was a trip of magnificent expectations, as they were directed to transport twice as much "booze," as the first time. Rewards were beginning to mount and it could not have been more welcome or appreciated.

Things proceeded smoothly for the first part. Upon leaving Georgia they encountered extremely heavy rain, between Tallahassee and Pensacola, Florida; raging torrents swept up from the Gulf of Mexico, necessitating a twenty minutes stop on the side of the road, underneath a patch of huge, old, Live Oak trees.

"What you gonna' do with your cut, Harry?"

"I'm going to put it in the bank, save it for a rainy day, like today. How about you?"

"I want to improve my business equipment, make my place the finest in the south," the little man responded.

"Peter Lou," offered, I'd like to open up a good Greek restaurant, there sure as Hell ain't one in town now!"

Rain subsided quickly as it came. Remainder was uneventful. Arriving in "sin city," all agreed to have French food, as that, too, was rare fare in town. "Peter Lou, don't you want to change that Restaurant from Greek to French?" "No, thank you, there ain't no French in Savannah, the only French I know is polyvoo franche, and that won't cut it."

Meeting went off as planned, vehicles loaded by three burly Italian guys, causing the rear of one vehicle to dip down somewhat, cargo carefully covered with canvas.

9

Wolfe was approached by two men, who escorted him to a tiny office at the rear of the warehouse. Whereupon he was introduced to Sylvestro "Sam" Carolla, the "first Boss of New Orleans outfit of Le Cosa Nostra." Cash counted and paid. Carolla transformed the "Family" from a simple extortion racket into a criminal enterprise making millions of dollars a year. He was, without a doubt the "bootlegging king" of New Orleans. He controlled it lock, stock and barrels. The New Orleans Police Department was there for him twenty-four hours a day, seven days a week. His control and influence was complete and absolute. If he ordered "it" to be done, "it" was done, no questions asked.

No one could challenge him, including Al Capone, whom in 1929 visited New Orleans to demand that Carolla supply him with booze, and quit supplying his chief rival in Chicago, Victor Aiello, but when Capone got off the train, Carolla had several police at his side, they completely disarmed Capone's bodyguards, and broke their fingers. Capone got the message, immediately re-boarded the train back to Chicago.

Naturally, the "little man" had no knowledge of this history or back ground, he was quite impressed and positively shaken when he received it. Nervous shivers ran down his spine, and the hair on the back of his neck curled up. "Jeeze," he murmured to himself.

During that brief conversation, Carolla made several memorable remarks: "This life of ours, this is a wonderful life. If you can get through life like this, and get away with it, hey, that's great. But it is very unpredictable."

"The only time you lie is when you are afraid!"

"Keep your friends close, but your enemies closer."

"Some people use the word MAFIA like they know what it means. They don't have any idea. Let me tell you.

Morte Alla Francia Italia Anelia. That's Italian for death to the French is Italy's cry. First letters of the verse are taken, the anagram MAFIA is deciphered. That word was first used in 1862 in a play by Giuseppi Rizzuto called *I Mafioso della Vicaria,* (The Mafia in the Village,) about a secret criminal group in prison of Palermo, Italy." While this explanation was unraveling, three additional vehicles backed into the warehouse and loaded with booze. Cash paid, hugs, kisses on each cheek, Italian embrace and blessings. Wolfe could not believe his eyes. Cash actually filled the sixteen inches deep drawer in the desk, where Carolla sat, while two ever present bodyguards hovered like silent servants.

"Hey, don't you fellows have time for a little relaxation, maybe some drinks, visit the ladies on Bourbon Street, or just enjoy my cities hospitality?" "No, I think we better be going now, got a long drive, I don't want the guys to get too tired. Maybe next time."

It was now late in the afternoon, sun setting over the broad Mississippi River, you could hear the bands starting to play that "Inimitable Dixieland Jazz," one club featured a young, black musician named Louis Armstrong, another, a white named Al Hirt. You can't help but wonder what ever happened to those two?

Before they got into high gear, the proceeding halted. They heard from far off the sounds of a marching band. The noise came closer, whistle sounded, a forty pieces brass band exploded with exciting, toe tapping, hand clapping, music.

Wolfe yelled out the window to a young couple standing at street side, "What in Hell is going on?" "We don't know, I don't think they want anybody to know, maybe it's a secret." Two youngsters, about eighteen years

11

of age, shouted, "It's a parade, I think it is some kind of a competition, maybe for Mardi Gras!"

One band was dressed in black tie and tails, while a second one comprised of sixty men, average age of fifty, dressed in purple pantaloons, wearing turbans with numerous ornaments attached thereto, playing some peculiar instruments with mysterious symbols. Behind the band came three men carrying aloft a giant gold banner proclaiming "YAARAB SHRINE TEMPLE from Atlanta, Georgia." Band and marchers carried out an Arabian motif, and in case anyone missed it, on a cart-borne bass drum, twelve feet in diameter, the same message was inscribed above "World's biggest bass drum!"

"Hooray," yelled a man, who appeared to have recognized one of the fellows wearing a turban. "What are you yelling for?" "Don't you think yelling is called for? I recognize the leader of the band, and he is doing a swell job!" "How would you know that? I can't recognize that noise as being music! What does he represent any how?" "That's a secret, only fellow Masons know."

The two band parade turned the corner, whistle sounded again, so-called music stopped. Further down the street another whistle shrilled, and the whole business began again, but this interval provided the loaded vehicles time to cross the street and resume their momentous trip.

"Man, I wish we had time to watch that competition, that battle between the bag pipes and trumpets ought to be fierce, I bet a fellow could lose his hearing, if he stood too close. Maybe next time!"

After having cleared the parade, the lead car stopped at Bourbon Street and Orleans Street intersection in the

French Quarter, with its beautiful wrought iron–balconied buildings, French Market and "Home of the Muffuletta Sandwich, *Central Grocery*." Italian owned, Italian operated for over fifty years, finest Italian grocery store in America. Three drivers met to discuss route of departure, and, as it was late in the afternoon, convoy speed, designation of lookouts. They agreed to proceed in a north-westerly direction along the Southern side of Lake Pontchartrain towards Metairie, thence north to Hammond, Louisiana, at maximum speed of forty miles per hour. However, everyone understood, as long as they were in New Orleans City Limits, speed not exceed twenty miles per hour. Safe, not sorry.

"Fellows, you know Sam Carolla highly recommended *Central Grocery*, for a little road food, so let's stop by, and get some to go."

Upon entering, they were cheerfully greeted by two Italians wearing aprons, and were completely overcome by the magnificent aroma that permeated the entire establishment. Absolutely mouth watering, appetite inviting. "I have never smelled anything like this in my life," Wolfe commented to the owner, "Sam Carolla recommended this to us, we want some Muffuletta Sandwiches to go. How do you make one?" "Well, it is an old family secret, but I will tell you." *"Parla Italiano?"* "No, I don't speak Italian." "O.K., here goes, first you take one, twenty four inch long French Baguette split lengthwise. Then you add twelve ounces assorted deli meats and cheeses, like Ham, Mortadella, Genoa Salami, Provolone and Mozzarella cheeses, top it off with one-quarter cup of Olive Salad, made only with finest extra virgin olive oil and olives from nowhere else but Italy or Sicily." Ten pound sack in hand filled with "nectar from the Gods," and twelve bottles of *Coca Cola* to go, they were ready to roll, "Let's get where we ain't. HI YO SILVER, AWAY!"

Emerging slowly from the "Quarter," vehicle head lights beaming as a precautionary matter, began to pick up momentum. Huge feeling of elation overcame the individuals, two in lead car began singing songs and telling stories, mostly lies, with great enthusiasm. "Sit back, relax and let's enjoy this," the little man said, as if he were going to tell "Moxie" a bed time story.

As fate would decree, contentment was short lived. Before you could say, "Jack Robinson," "Moxie" blurted out, "Wolfie, I see three cars right behind us, slow down and let them pass." "Alright, we're not in any hurry, and this road ain't the best." Extending his left arm out the driver's side window, promptly gave the universal signal to slow down, "I sure don't want to do anything to attract attention, these three look like they're in a hurry, or something." "Come on, jackasses, the road is yours...I got all day and half the night..." The lead car decreased speed immediately, although followers blew their horns in impatience and disgust.

"Well, Moxie, it's a good thing you were watching so closely, I never would've seen them, sorta like they came up from out of nowhere, I'm not even sure they had lights on!"

"Wolfie, watch out! That damn fool is driving like a maniac, it looks like he wants to run us over!"

"I'll be damned, that's something, can't be too careful drivin' these strange roads."

In a very few moments, what had been a pleasant driving experience northward, suddenly was transformed into hell on earth. Alarm, confusion, upset simultaneously seized the driver; palms of his hands wet, face beaded in perspiration, ultimately terror set in causing him to gag, almost vomit.

"Man, you look how I feel, God awful terrible, I could puke!"

Driver's attention turned instantly to what was happening to his left, "Moxie's" observation and exclamation went un-answered. "This sure don't look too good; I've heard that the Ku Klux Klan operates all over this part of Louisiana, and they are a law unto themselves! People have been known to disappear without leaving a trace, they say, if the snakes and skeeters don't get ya' the alligators will!"

"Oh, my God, we're sure in for some strange going on's!" Next few minutes were the longest in Wolfe's life and forever sear his memory and burn a permanent scar on his mind. Always and always, from this day forward, it would eternally haunt him.

Pulling out on the left of the caravan, first of three cars sounded a siren while cutting without warning, directly in front of Wolfe's Packard "Eight." A man brandishing a pistol in his right hand, hanging out the right front side window, screaming to the top of his lungs, "Pull over, now, or I'll blow your damn brains out!" All this sudden, unexpected assault caused Wolfe to hit the brakes, slide off the roadway to his right. Two accompanying cars, each with four men, pulled in front of the two trucks, forcing immediate stops. The "Savannah Six," were stunned, shocked and alarmed as twelve occupants in three unmarked cars hit the ground running, rifles, shotguns and pistols drawn, groups of four approaching each Georgia vehicle.

"Get out with your hands up," one who assumed leadership, yelled in direction of the lead car. "Put your hands on the hood, and don't move, unless you want new holes in your asses!"

"Whoa, fellow, we ain't got no guns, and we ain't broke no speed limits!"

"Well, let me see what you got here, I sure hope it ain't nothin' illegal, cause we frown on law breakers of any kind!"

"Peter Lou," having regained his sensibilities, inquired, "Who are you any way? What's this all about?"

"We are City of New Orleans certified police officers, and I am Lieutenant Donald Nasworthy, my friends call me Nasty!" This six foot, six inches tall, two hundred fifty pounds of solid "red neck," looked every bit the part of a professional football defensive lineman, standing next to Wolfe, he just had to laugh, saying, "Little boy, where's your mama?"

The other eleven began pushing the occupants aside, after a quick pat down for weapons told them, "Get your dirty asses over there, and don't say one damn word!"

"Now sir, we don't aim to cause no trouble; we are all from Savannah, Georgia, and never been in any trouble with the law before. You can call the Chief of Police there and he will tell you that."

"Well, that sure is nice, but you may be in some now!" Opening the rear door of the "Eight," Lt. Nasworthy exclaimed, "My goodness, what have we here, looks like a nice stack of canvas; I wonder if it's covering up any thing?"

"Gollee, there is some barrels under there, what in the world could possibly be in these nice barrels? Sorghum? Water? Why, Hell, they sure smell strange!" Beckoning to his assistant, Sgt. Thurman Faircloth, also a huge white man, "Get a hammer and axe, let's see and taste what's in there." Faircloth, running excitedly to his car, said, "I'll be right back Lieutenant, I haven't run this far since I played football in high school!" Returning promptly, he questioned the group, "What you fellas got in there? It might save time if you just tell us." "Sir, I can't be sure, all I is, is a delivery boy, and these five are my friends," Wolfe quietly remarked.

"Crap! Do I look like a moron to you? You don't expect me to believe that crap, do you?"

"Mister, I'm telling it like it is, we are just delivery boys."

Rolling one keg outside the car, Faircloth motioned to two others, "Set it up right, I don't want to lose none!" One tap of the hammer on top of the keg produced desired results, booze trickled out. "I'll be damned, if that ain't some kind of alkeyhall, or white lightening. Don't know which, but I do know it ain't legal, and, you boys done stepped into a high pile of doo-doo!"

"I got no choice but to ask you six to get in our cars, and we will all go back for a little ride to New Orleans! Faircloth, you and two others drive them vehicles, bring them to the old car barn, where we will meet. Don't get lost and don't make any stops on the way!"

Reality, terror began to settle in the minds of six very tired, very scared Georgia boys, it all seemed so unreal, so impossible, so completely unbelievable. Minds turned numb, stomachs tightened into knots, sweat flowed from every pore. "Damn, what we gonna do now? Strangers in a strange land, with no body to turn to, and not much money to turn a deal with."

17

"Think hard, pray a lot, your whole life is staring you square in your face, and getting' out is a helluvah lot harder than getting' in!"

"God, please have mercy on us!"

"Bub" Lennahan, lookout in the second truck, was high strung and nervous by nature. Little, five foot, eight inches tall Irishman took pride in his heritage, "that's L-E-N-N-A-H-A-N, and that's real Irish, anyone with three N's in their last name, is real Irish, not one of them pretend Irish." A meal a day was plenty for him, existing on black coffee, "weighing in at one hundred twelve pounds." Talkative, he was "Old Fort Irish," growing up in a neighborhood not too far from "Wolfie," and one of the very few people, outside his immediate family that called him "Wolfie."

"Wolfie, this here thing can be real serious, but I got my faith in God, and trust in you."

Arriving at the appointed meeting place, "Six" were herded into a small room, with a decided odor of gasoline or fuel oil, near one designated "OFFICE." Directed to "sit down, keep your mouths shut, and Lieutenant will see you shortly, one at a time. We aim to get to the bottom of this."

"We must agree to let Wolfe do the talking, cause we don't know nothing about nothing, that way we won't cross each other up," Harry suggested, his beard darkened Greek countenance, fairly glowing with perspiration.

"That's fine with me," "Moxie" chimed in, "I never was much good at talkin' and Wolfe is a good talker, 'cause he done talked all us into this." That produced some laughter in the group, breaking the tension.

Ten minutes elapsed, door opened, Corporal Purdue, pointing toward "Bub" in a solemn manner, wheezed, "Let's talk to that skinny little runt over there first, then, if he can't help us, we will talk to you," pointing at Wolfe, "next."

"Bub" left the room, skipping along like a school girl on her first day at class. "Sir, can I please go Pee?"

"O.K., but don't take all day!"

Returning to the "Office," he strictly adhered to the line, except adding, "That's L-E-N-N-A-H-A-N, real Irish, good Catholic, used to be an altar boy, worked in Sacred Heart Church as a part time janitor. Never been in trouble, am an only child, you can check me out with the Chief of Police in Savannah, he'll tell you I'm O. K. Just here for a ride, that's all, and don't know nothin' else."

"Alright, we understand, go on back, we'll get to the next guy in a minute."

Walls between the two rooms were thin enough so that voices were easily overheard. One of the Sergeant's stated, "That's pretty good stuff they got there, I'd know those barrels any where." Another suggested, "Check them out in Savannah, let me know what's what. Leave 'em coolin' their heels for now."

"Alright, you nice people, before we talk to anyone else, we're gonna check with authorities in Savannah, so stay where you are, we'll see you later. Door closed, lock clicked, and a guard posted nearby.

"Bub, you did good, we're all proud of you. Now, let's get some rest, we'll need it."

Two hours later, deprived of food and water, the door popped open, revealing the imposing statue of Lieutenant "Nasty." "O. K., next," pointing at Wolfe. Struggling to his feet after sitting on the floor, departed, walking slowly, without hesitation, "Yes, sir." "Sir, look, I hope you checked us out; ain't none of us ever been in trouble before, we got no money, neither have any of our families."

19

"Who's Packard is that?"

"Mine."

"How did you get that, it's expensive!"

"I put eight hundred down, owe the rest, the payment receipt book is in the compartment, I've got twenty-four more months to pay on it, at Chatham Savings and Loan."

"Where'd you get that booze? Don't lie, I think I know."

"Sir, we picked it up at a warehouse downtown from a guy whose name is Sam."

"Who do you work for?"

"Nobody, I'm just a delivery boy, we are supposed to get our orders once we reach Jackson, Mississippi. This, is our first trip, I spent everything I had to set it up."

"Well, I'm truly sorry about that, my heart bleeds for you; 'cause we want the booze, trucks and your Packard. Think it over, when you are ready to talk, knock on the door...don't take too long, as all we had to eat was those Mufulletas...man, that's good eatin'."

Silently he withdrew to rejoin his friends, who, for the most part overheard the entire discussion.

"Those dirty bastards, ate our food," Harry moaned.

"Shhh, let's think. The Bank wants that Packard, if I can't pay for it; it's almost new; they'll take it back, so, maybe we can give up everything else, and hopefully get out of here."

Knock, knock.

"Can I speak to Lieutenant, please?"

"He's not here, I can get him, it' ll take a minute."

Thirty minutes later "Nasty" shows up, conference was short and sweet. "Sir, we'll give you every thing we got, except the Packard, which the bank holds the papers on, and $65.00 to get us back to Georgia...you'll never see us again, under any set o' circumstances; we will agree never to set foot in Louisiana again, ever, as long as we live! We are all poor as can be, you know how bad business has been in this depression, no jobs, nothin'. Please, you will not regret this, besides, I got to pay for those two trucks! God-a- mighty, I don't know how!"

"I'll think about it...see you tomorrow...guard, see that they get one loaf of bread, one gallon o' water...no visitors, no calls."

"Can't we call home?"

"Hell, no!"

Wolfe returned to the holding room, strain vividly shown on his youthful face. "Boys, I did my best, played all my cards, wait and see."

"It's strange we ain't in jail..."

"This is worse than jail, no bed, no chair, nothin'..."

"So, whose complaining...?"

"Sleep tight."

As the tiny room darkened, Harry, face expressionless, murmurs forlornly, "God, please have mercy on us...Bub, say some prayers for all o' us."

"Bub" sat up straight and important like, his thin, homely, little, milk colored face strained with excitement, and immense anxiety, sharp green eyes glancing from side to side taking in everything; the sudden quiet, creaking of an old door and impending darkness. He wanted to weep, but silently, without tears, because he had good common sense that no one would notice or comfort him.

"Holy Mary, Mother of God, pray for us now!"

"Thanks."

"I'm just sittin' here, not feelin' anything; not even sad, cause all at once I know I can sit here now and forever and laugh until salty tears roll down my cheeks into the corners

21

of my mouth...live while you live, then die and be done with it."

Day break comes early in south Louisiana, heralded in by the loud voice of Corporal Purdue, "Good morning ladies, hope you had a good night's rest...here, I brought you coffee and corn bread, try not to leave any left-overs. Lieutenant will be here in about two hours to talk to you," pointing at Wolfe, "I know you been lookin' forward to that, that'll make you happy. Try not to impress him with your intelligence, given the mess you in."

"No, sir, I'm sure he knows that already, I can only hope he understands and that he'll be considerate of us."

"If it's consideration you're lookin' for, you come to the wrong place. We are fresh out o' consideration, and not likely to get in a new supply any time soon. Consider yourself fortunate... consideration... what a joke!" "Man, what I wouldn't give for a bath, hot meal and a good night's sleep; you sure don't miss the honey 'till the bees are gone, rings true. Well, we don't have too much longer to wait."

Lieutenant "Nasty" arrived a little late, really full of himself, ready to take on the world, like a duck on a June Bug.

"Alright, little boy, come on in, and let's talk a little. I don't have a lot of time to waste, so I'll get right to it. We checked, and you told it right, no body got any criminal records, all of you been long time residents of Savannah. God only knows why, but that is your tough luck, six no bodies from no where, what a treat this is for us."

"Sir, we are all sorry as we can be for this mess, we sure have learned our lessons."

"Well, the good news is that I will take your offer, however, you will have to sign some papers, then we'll be

22

done with you. You got one hour to clear out of this parish, make no mistakes, one of my men will be following you. Don't stop for any reason, just get the Hell out of here, remember, we do not want to see your sorry asses back here in Louisiana, ever, I mean never! Do you understand that? If so, then go tell your buddies, see if they have any questions. If anyone doesn't like it, then, I got the jail bus outside with six empty seats."

"Sir, all I can say is thank you."

In the next room, five men rose to their feet as if ordered to do so by some superior officer, standing erect, eyes filled with blank stares, expecting the worse. Each appearing as though they were awaiting the hangman's noose. Wolfe began slowly, repeating every word he had heard, following it up by asking if there were any questions. Hearing none, turned to "Nasty," nodded O. K.

Within five seconds, all six men climbed into the Packard, anxious to follow Lieutenant down town to Police Headquarters. Located in the heart of the business district, next to the U. S. Court House, that shabby, worn down, old building was indeed a sight for sore eyes. The Plaza Hotel could not be more inviting. Each man was carefully identified in one folder, given the final warning, "Not one of you is welcome here in the City of New Orleans; do not return, remember, drive straight out of town, no stops for any reason whatsoever. You got that?"

In unison, they nodded affirmatively, smiled faintly, said "Thank you, sir."

Six tired but happy men entered that Packard quickly, smallest first, as there was only one bench like front seat. "We will have to take turns sitting up here," Wolfe stated quietly, "I want to thank you all, I really appreciate your stickin' together, I hope when we get back to town, that I can make it up to you some day."

"Wolfe, you know, we are all three times seven, we knew what we were doing, some times you got to take the bitter with the sweet," Harry responded, "too bad it didn't work out, but one thing is for sure, I am damn glad we got out with all our fingers and toes."

"Thank God for all favors!"

The first one hundred miles was traveled in complete silence, punctuated only by snoring sounds emitting from three men in the back of the sedan.

Harry, who was oldest, sat next to Wolfe who was driving, said in a whispered tone, "You know, we were really quite fortunate getting' out of that mess, I was beginning to worry...how do you feel?"

"Man, I don't know. That whole situation bothered me from the start, I'd like to kick it around with you, if you feel up to it?" "Sure, lay it out."

"I'm thinking, I was set-up, and knocked over like a game of ten pins, it was too damn smooth. We did nothin' to attract attention, but we were stopped before we got out of town. When Sam Carolla told me that he and Capone were not friends, and, that he actually had Capone's body guards' fingers broken, on their first visit to New Orleans, my blood ran cold. I did not know that, had no way of knowing that, and it was all about Carolla's failure to supply Capone booze. I thought I'd have a heart attack right on the spot."

"For crissake Wolfe, that is awful! We are mighty damn lucky to have walked out of there, we could've all been busted up badly."

"I want to think about this, so let's keep it quiet for the time being. I sure as Hell don't want to be involved in a war between those two guys…try to get some sleep, 'cause I want you to relieve me in four hours."

That idea haunted him every day of his life, he was never able to determine the real truth about his suspicion.

Upon returning home, he was greeted by family and friends. After revealing the events of the earlier days, one friend casually remarked: "Little Bo Peep lost his sheep." That nickname stuck his entire lifetime. Known by one and all. This man of small statue, five feet, five inches tall; weighed approximately 150 pounds on his best day; wore black horn-rimmed eye glasses, black hair, green eyes, and all man. Nothing, nor no one scared "Bo."

"Bo Peep's Billiard Parlor," was located adjacent to the *Savannah Hotel*, one of the three decent hotels in town; across Congress Street from the *Christ Church*. A restaurant provided twelve delicious items, but the roast beef sandwich was the best that any man ever tasted. White bread piled high with the finest roast beef money could buy from *Armour's Meat Packing Co.*, flown in from Chicago, Illinois, covered with rich, thick, brown gravy, so magnificently tasty, it brought tears of joy to your eyes. The kind your Mother wished she could make, served on ceramic dishes adorned with a sheep's likeness, that became his trade mark. No paper plates nor plastic dinner ware.

Cast of characters that worked in the establishment, was very interesting, to say the least. "Bo" was boss, but John D. "Tiger" Ware, was manager, book-keeper, check writer and good Irish Catholic, that attended church daily. A large framed, big shoulder man, weighed about 200 pounds, never smiled, always a *Havana-Tampa Cigar* stuck, unlit in his mouth, chewed upon it until it was a nub. Of course, he spit tobacco juice in the waste basket located behind him and to his left.

"Johnny" Ware was "Savannah born, Savannah bred, and when I die, I'll be Savannah dead." He received his education in the parochial school system, graduated from Benedictine Military School. A good man from a good family. He and his wife Mary were proud of their two children, a daughter and a son, Jerry, who entered the priesthood, perhaps the happiest day of their lives. Possessor of an interesting and unique attribute in that he could conduct two conversations in person, at the same time, a third on the telephone, neither missing a word, nor requiring repetition. Which certainly came in handy when being confronted with hearing impaired Meyer.

Quiet, polite, soft spoken, hardly ever raised his voice, and never used profanity or curse words. On the rare occasion that he became upset or angry, remark, "And to think I gave up a promising career with C & S Bank, to work here. I should have my head examined." "You wouldn't work anywhere else, you know we couldn't get along without you," Meyer quickly responded, "It'll take an army of accountants to straighten out the mess you got them books in!"

"Tiger" maintained two bank accounts, one for "operating expense," the other for "cash reserves," and became a past master explaining the two to "Bo," who had difficulty understanding the difference, - "They both money, ain't they?"

In the early days he bragged that he was quite an athlete. Write a check, give it to a merchant, and then run to the bank to cover it with a deposit. "Man, they thought Jesse Owens was fast, molasses compared to me!"

"Tiger" was quite a fellow. A real original, personality like none other. Gruff, deliberate, patient, loyal and fair in all his business dealings. He proudly proclaimed that he, "Kept the ship afloat," handling every day finances, check writing, bank deposits and the like. He visited the Citizens and Southern National Bank, prior to 2:00 P.M. close, it was rumored, he told them not to close before he got there. Mills B. Lane himself sat, watch in hand, awaiting his arrival, then signaled the armed guard to close the huge iron doors behind him.

"Johnny's" most precious possession was a broad point *Parker* real ink pen, not one of those cheap ball point types. He kept it filled with black permanent ink, located in his coat pocket next to his heart, for his exclusive use. Don't ask to write with that pen, nobody. Always dressed in a coat and white shirt with dark colored necktie, he solely was responsible for maintaining the business checking account and payment of bills. The loose leaf style check book, three checks to a page, stubs for record keeping attached.

Occasionally deliveries were made requiring payment on receipt, or C. O. D. Herein lies another tale. The procedure was unique and absolutely astounding: "What you got there?" "Bill for chairs." "Leave it, I will take care of it." "No, sir, I have to get a check." "Well, can't you see I'm busy, you'll have to wait." "Okay." Ten minutes later, "Sir, I have to go, can I have a check now?" "Tiger" bit down on the ever present cigar, moving it from the right to the left side of his mouth, take check book out, open it on the counter, put on his green book keeper's visor, look carefully at recipient, withdraw pen, unscrew cap, placing it upon pen, transfer it from left to right hand, raise his right arm, not unlike a pitcher on the mound in his

27

windup, flex right arm, place right hand upon check book, smooth writing surface, look again at recipient, clear his throat, lean over check book, make three circular motions, pen in right hand, in preparation to write. The entire procedure took several minutes, was duplicated every check. In the meanwhile, that poor fellow waiting, became so damn mad, he'd say something like, "For crissake, I got to go!" Request fell on deaf ears. He was truly fortunate that the telephone didn't ring, otherwise, he'd suffer through a re- enactment. Upon receipt, guy bit his tongue, "Thanks a lot!" through clinched teeth. Responding, in like manner, "Tiger" gave him one of his familiar "Chessie-cat grins." No joviality intended.

Then, there was Meyer Pinzer, short, fat, Jew, nose like Jimmy Durante; stuttered, hard of hearing, talked with a slight "Yankee" accent; head cashier, over looked activities in the "pool room." While standing at the cash register, amused himself playing piano on register keys. Answered telephone in a loud voice, "Bo Peep's Billiard Parlor!" "Who, Johnny Fruckles?" Yell, "Is Johnny Fruckles in the house?" If so, and didn't want to be disturbed, shake his head no. Frequently, the person called stood within a few feet of Meyer, but that did not deter him from yelling. All these actions to the delight of spectators.

The atmosphere was unbelievable. Doctors, lawyers, merchants, politicians, rich, poor, Irish, Jew or "Cracker," came in during the day, and into the night, until mid-night closing. A man could get a beer, drink of whiskey at the bar in the rear, just over 100 feet from *Christ Church*, to comply with law; a great meal, whether fried shrimp, shrimp Creole, hamburger, grilled cheese, whatever suits a man's fancy.

Whereas, "Tiger" lived up to his nick-name, pacing behind the cigar counter with a scowl on his face, head set squarely on shoulders, never smiling, very much as a Tiger does in a cage; Meyer was a different breed of cat, he was just plain Meyer, more like a pussycat. A butcher of the English language; "Mabo," for Mobile; "Detrout," for Detroit; "Indiansana for Indiana; "Heintz," for Hiers; any proper name was fair game, and did it without a smile, was it intentional? Who knows, somehow it seemed to fit. Employed there at an early age, at his brother's request, became a trusted employee. He'd tell a story, punctuated with stuttering, place his left hand behind his ear to assist hearing, laugh out loud at his story in a shrill, staccato, "Ha, Ha, Ha." Proud, without profanity; gentleman; strong as an ox. While listening to someone he did not believe, pursed his lips as though tasting a sour lemon, stare intently at the speaker as if he had three noses. Rarely anyone took offense, as they understood he was acting. Nobody was safe from his pranks. Customers inquired, "Did I get any calls?" Responded, "Yes, two, one from your psychiatrist, another from your wife, she said eat out 'cause she is playing Bridge and won't be home 'till next week!" Or, "No, we just take important calls!" Followed by that "hysterical" laughter. Unquestionably, he loved "Bo Peep," that business and it's inhabitants, arrived early for his shift that began at 11:30 A.M., sat in front of the cash register, do nothing until the precise time. If the phone rang, pretended not to hear, asked to answer, retorted, "No, I'm not on duty now;" close his eyes, act as though asleep, including exaggerated snoring sounds. What a guy.

Another favorite trick frequently involved customers standing, watching games of pool. Meyer approached from behind and to their right, quietly; tap them on the left shoulder, move quickly away, as the person looked to his left to see who tapped him. Meyer roared with laughter as though it was the funniest thing he had ever seen; elbow others to attract attention, point at the victim, all the while making his familiar lip pursing expression, clap hands and mimic the unsuspecting fellow. Infinitely funnier than "The Three Stooges."

Most of the times the prank was well received, everyone enjoying a good laugh. But, as you might expect, not all the time.

Arthur Sternshine, long time clerk at *Morris Levy's Store for Men,* about sixty years of age, tall, slim, elegant, quiet, immaculately dressed, groomed to perfection. Indeed a gentleman's gentleman. Unassuming, self respecting, speak when spoken to, and only in the most polite manner. Well, that is, until Meyer pulled that "dastardly deed," on him. Nine witnesses saw it all, the ensuing spontaneous laughter was loud. Seems like everybody enjoyed it but Arthur, who was "mad as Hell," and not going to take it at all, having spilled coffee on his beautiful silk jacket, tie and pants.

"Are you crazy..." he screeched, "have you lost your mind? I do not appreciate being the butt of your crass humor, I demand to see Johnny Ware or Bo Peep himself!" Just so happened that both of them had seen the future, and ran out the front door together, advising "Stuffy" Ennis to "take care of everything until we return. You are in charge!" It was a good thing that Arthur had to go to work, departing before our heroes re-entered. Results; Meyer got the dry cleaning bill.

Will Rogers is usually credited with the expression, "I never met a man I didn't like." That may be true, however, the "little man " acquired it, as one rule of life or code of conduct. He absolutely loved people. Employer-employee relationship was unique. Hiring was his province, and whenever it became necessary, which was almost never, the firing as well. "Bo" and "Tiger," were friends right from the start. Not a single day passed without frequent, earnestly solicited consultations, and input. Eyeball to eyeball, serious, quiet discussions in almost a reverential tone. Each utilized their "nick names," with smiles on their respective faces. They simply would not permit a discourteous act or word to pass between them, nor engage in impolite conduct of any nature. Two men of such incredibly diverse back- grounds working together in complete harmony was remarkable to say the very least, especially, given the fact, they both were very emotional. Whenever a personal trouble arose, each responded without delay, and as expected; knowing the other, they sensed unhappiness immediately. If a financial problem confronted either, a speedy solution was achieved. Harmony prevailed over twenty-five years during their relationship. Few, if any businessmen can make that statement truthfully.

Meyer was treated in a like manner, although his duties and responsibilities were vastly different. Daily, he and "Bo" talked about anything and everything from baseball to zoos, always warmly and sincerely. He had a genuine feeling of love and caring for children, which, obviously, was returned. A born comedian, could make anyone laugh with his antics, personality and remarks.

Meyer was a "favorite uncle," to "Bo's" boys. Provider of chewing gum, ready to slip a dime or quarter when the children ran to see him. He lived alone in a one bed room apartment not far from the business, walked to and from daily. Good "husband material," but, with his speech impediment and hearing disability, believed that he was not attractive.

These three men were responsible for the routine operation of that business. All told, Meyer worked there nineteen years, until he died.

Loyalty. That was the whole fabric that covered this group. "To obtain loyalty, you must give loyalty." Their love and respect, each for the other was supreme. No one could ever speak ill of one in presence of another. "Do not speak of him in that manner, in my presence. I do not appreciate it;" or, "Hey, fellow, watch your mouth!" Other employees understood that, also knew that all they had to do was their job, if so, they had a job for life. "Bo Peep" hated to fire anybody, it pained him greatly, about the only way one could be fired was to be beyond redemption, absolute lost cause, hopeless. In all his years, only three people earned that "distinction," and when it was over, he gave them two weeks pay! He'd carry the grief home, explain it to any listener. It made him utterly miserable. One long- time employee was a "cripple," as result of a broken back incurred as a teenager; had posture of a "question mark." Unemployable to all, except "Bo;" who not only employed him, but also retained him for over fifteen years. Human kindness, over flowing! As *Shakespeare* wrote in *"Macbeth," "Yet I do fear thy nature; It is too full o' the milk of human kindness."*

Rabbi George M. Solomon, Temple Mickve Israel, served as friend and confidant of the three. Over forty years he was the "Chief fund raiser, bottle washer," a self proclaimed, apt description. When the Temple needed a "major" contribution, he called at 19 East Congress. Warmly welcomed, with most precious words to any fund raiser's ears, "Your request is my command." 1942 through 1950 were very good years for "Bo Peep," in turn, it was good years for the Temple. Dr. Solomon appreciated his generosity to such a degree that he personally recommended that a beautiful stained glass window be dedicated and installed in the Temple sanctuary, "To Wolfe W. Silver and his Wife," in recognition of his "permanent endowment."

Loyalty, Dedication, Generosity, should appear as well.

Exact same report can be made of B. B. Jacob Synagogue, where Rabbi A. I. Rosenberg presided for years. It was not unusual for him to call for a contribution, then come pick it up in person. In appreciation, he too, sponsored a resolution to dedicate a stained glass window in the sanctuary. That beautiful old synagogue was later abandoned and sold, after the congregation decided to move to south side of town. Where are those beautiful stained glass windows now? Who knows? "Only the Shadow knows!"

Loyalty, Dedication, Generosity!

"He was too good for his own good." "He was a bridge over troubled waters," are but two descriptions most frequently heard of this "little man."

God, don't you know, "He was his brother's keeper, and his sister's, too."

One of the really nice aspects about that business was at any time the doors were open, someone could be found to talk with. Clean rest rooms, immaculate kitchen, lunch counter so clean people said "you could eat off the floor." Winter, it was heated by steam heat rising from silver painted radiators maintained at a comfortable 72 degrees. Summer, cooled by the largest air conditioner in town, also at a pleasant 71 degrees. Clean, fresh air was pumped in, so that odor of tobacco was removed quickly. Port of call for salesman from all over the country, eager to display their wares of neck ties to diamond rings, and everything in between. Always something or somebody was going on, an atmosphere never created before or since. Tourists staying at *Savannah Hotel,* next door, were directed there by bell boys and bell captain, or as some prefer "Doorman." Taxi drivers recommended the location freely, without hesitation, because they knew that "every thing was alright." Everyone was made to feel "at home." No pretensions, no phoniness, no guile.

Lucca Brazzi, a regular visitor from Brooklyn, New York, said, "When I die, I don't want to go to heaven, I want to go to Bo Peep's." His partner, Sal "The Finger" Lucchese, got his nickname because every word he uttered, was punctuated on the listener's chest, with an extended index finger. His claim to fame was once he attended mass, walked forward to receive communion from the Bishop at St. Patrick's Cathedral in New York, his pistol fell out of his "underarm holster," causing considerable embarrassment and consternation by all.

Loneliness is a terrible thing, even for a guy from Brooklyn. Sal and Lucca were two really tough guys. Every thing about them sent signals and warnings. Their attitude, persona, bearing. Each weighed about two hundred sixty pounds, dark hair, eyes, complexion; six feet tall; big heads, shoulders, waist lines, hands, arms, mouths. Reputed to be "collectors" for one of the "major crime families in New York," "extortionists," the U. S. Attorney called them in a sixteen count indictment. "Enforcers," others said. Regardless, while in town, they were "pussy cats." Two weeks they actually lived in "Bo Peep's," not going out doors one time. "Ain't nothin' goin' on out there any way. New York, this ain't." They occupied three seats in front of the counter, across from "Tiger" and Meyer. Carefully reviewing the *New York Times*, enabled them to stay abreast of "what was happening in the Big Apple." No telephone calls in or out. An unexpected thing about them was they were funny. Yes, funny. Something like this, "Hey, Morrie, what is happening? Where you been? Still goin' to that Catholic school wearing those play soldier suits? You been goin' there now, at least six years I know, how long its goin' to take you to matrickalate? "Look here, I was readin' in the newspaper that two bodies were found in an abandoned car...any body caught sleepin' in a trunk of a car, ought to get shot." "When we goin' to eat some Italian food? Pasta, lasagna, rigatonis, pizzas, canolis, all at one sitting! We been hungry for a week." "Look at Tiger, he got a face only his mother could love. He wears drawers made of flour sacks, he's so damn cheap." Meyer is hilarious, he's the only guy I know that laughs at his own jokes. I wish I had his nose filled with nickels, I'd be rich!" On and on, un-relenting, two colorful characters.

Early in the development of his business, "Bo" determined to offer the best, highest quality, tastiest food; reasonably priced, that could be found in Savannah. It was his passion, one principal to which, he dedicated his life. Searching the town for a "luncheonette manager," was an arduous task, but he was up to it. In those days, many of the good restaurants were owned and operated by Greeks, so, he concentrated there. Several interviews were conducted until he met one Chris Vatsios, an outstanding chef in his own right, owner of a restaurant on Bull Street for five years. "I want you to run my luncheonette, provide the most delicious food, money can buy; I want it spotlessly clean, at the same time economical. Food is merely an attraction, I will make my money on the pool tables. You can't eat them, they don't get stale, they're no overhead.!" "Mister, you got your man, salary plus a small percentage, I will start in ten days," Chris responded in his best Greek dialect. Gentleman, congenial, master chef with Greek influence, devotion to duty, that was a match made in heaven. Arriving early, about five thirty, he prepared the menu and food for that particular day, fresh, something new, different, featuring twenty five items. That was fine for a while, then "Bo" altered the menu after consultation with "Tiger," reducing it to twelve regular, reliable, man satisfying dishes, every day except Friday, that being "fish day," when the town's best "Shrimp Creole," was featured, posting a hand written note inside the cellophane menu cover, "SPECIAL," today only, fresh Shrimp Creole on a bed of white rice, only $1.95, bread or rolls, drink included. (Circa 1935.) Absolutely, positively, delicious, spicy sauce. None better, anywhere! Large, tender Georgia Shrimp, delivered fresh off the shrimp boat by Frank C. Mathews, Sr., owner of *"Mathew's Fish Market,"* on Congress Street, near the old City Market, three blocks west. Savannah's finest fish and seafood purveyor for many years, until his health became impaired, succeeded by Frank C. Mathews, Jr., who continued the same fine tradition until retirement. That was "some triple play, Jew to Greek from Italian." Can you beat that sports fans? No! Hell, No!

It was under Vatsios' regime the "World Famous Roast Beef Sandwich," was developed. After several years of service, determined to "return to homeland, live out remainder of my years." That decision was not unexpected, as his health steadily declined. Prior to departure, assisted "Bo" every way to employ a successor. Two weeks later, a black man, John J. Jackson was named "Chef in Charge," student under Vatsios for several weeks.

36

"I'm ready, Boss," he said with a mile wide grin, "John J. Jackson is here to serve you, now! Yessir, make no mistake about it, history will be made, the food will exceed the grade, the best for less, and, no mess, just you wait and see!" Six feet, six inches tall, one hundred seventy five pounds, light skin, black man, with a charming attitude, and ability to prepare some really tasty food. Trained at two New York restaurants, before returning home to Savannah. He, like his predecessor, arrived early, six days a week, prepared the food, fresh "from scratch;" dressed in immaculate, long, white apron, white shirt, shoes, pants, and tall "stovepipe chef's hat," making him appear nine feet tall. An imposing figure of a man. Good student, he thoroughly learned everything there was to know about roast beef, its purchase and preparation. First and foremost was the meat was AAA, Grade One, Prime, direct from Chicago, Illinois, through *Armour Meat Company*. Not less than forty pounds of prime cut especially to "Bo's" specifications. No waste, gristle or fat. Individually wrapped in heavy duty brown butcher's paper, enclosed in string net type fabric. Roasted in oven, in it's natural juices, at a temperature not to exceed three hundred degrees, visually observed using unique glass window, monitored for texture, flavor and tenderness. Removed from oven, in stainless steel pan, placed upon a heat unit, that maintained its constant temperature. Gravy, thick brown gravy, most flavorful ever tasted by human mankind, kept separately in another stainless steel pot nearby. Aroma of that still permeates the atmosphere, worth a pound of gold, make a hungry man drool. Never before, or since, has anyone even closely approached the taste of that magnificent gourmet treat. Bar none! Stuff

37

served today called "roast beef" tastes like cardboard in comparison.

Watching Jackson approach that huge mound of beef, with sixteen inch razor sharp knife in right hand, indispensable knife sharpener in left, upon which he repeatedly stroked and honed it, was indeed something to behold. Solemn ritual, serious as the well known "heart attack." First slice off the top was always set aside, should the "Boss, need to taste it." Anyone who ever experienced that taste sensation remembers it forever, and ever. "That is one helluvah treat, if I could bottle that aroma, I'd be rich; if Jackson was a woman, I'd marry him," "Marvelous Marvin" Cohen remarked; "Me, too," "Sleepy" Wagman added. The legend grew and grew.

The entire Congress Street front of the building was huge glass windows, adorned with a hand painted likeness of a white sheep, approximately five feet wide by five feet high, emblazoned across the image was BO PEEP'S in bright red letters. A design masterpiece neon sign hung in the middle of the front, twenty feet off street level. It, too, was huge. Twenty-two feet high, eleven feet wide, bright green, twelve inches red and white letters, outlined in green and pink neon. When it was erected in 1935, it was reputed to be the largest NEON sign in town; proclaimed to all the world, BO PEEP'S Billiard Parlor and Restaurant, 19 E. Congress Street, THE FINEST IN THE SOUTH. Extending perpendicular from the building, remained in place until the property was sold in 1955. Easily visible no matter which way one approached, as both sides were duplicates. Constructed with Savannah Grey Brick, covered with smooth finish stucco, painted light pastel green. Due to ridiculous town ordinance, two separate entrances were required, two double glass doors, wood frames; one to the restaurant, the other to pool room, so that minors could enter restaurant, without going into pool room, conveniently enabling some dads who desired to "shoot a little pool," while son was partaking of some delicious repast. On rare occasions, father quietly" instructed son, "Now don't forget what I told you to tell your Mother, if she asks where you been? Say, we had lunch at Leopold's." "O. K., but will you take me to get ice cream at Leopold's? I love ice cream!" "Yes, I guess that can be arranged. I like their ice cream too."

Then, of course one could make a wager or bet with "Bo" for "Any amount that you can count, on any game that you can name!" "Don't worry about the mule being blind, just load the wagon!" College and professional football, basketball, or baseball, and, if the ponies were "your poison," you could bet on any horse race, any where in the country. He had every post time, at the conclusion, knew results of the race immediately after they crossed the finish line. If a sporting event was broadcast, "Bo" had it. He sat in his favorite chair, next to customers, silently rooting for his favorite team, or the one with which he'd prosper most. Now, this was contrary to law, but "Bo" had "a way" with local law enforcement, lawyers and politicians. At one point in time, it was estimated he had as many law enforcement types on his "payroll," as the town. Always good for a free meal, cigars, cash loan, charity contribution. He knew them all, and they all knew him when they were in need. A popular saying was, "The Irish run Savannah; the Jews own it; and the Crackers enjoy it!"

There was a fifteen foot long black board behind cigar counter, where "Tiger" worked, upon which all sports scores were constantly recorded. Information was provided by *Western Union Ticker Service*, which produced a thin yellow tape of all information, such as pitchers, runs, hits, errors, home run hitters. Many of the most prominent men in town placed bets, sit and listen to the game, or watch the tape. Meyer would yell, "In the fifth at New York, DiMaggio hit home run, one on!" Then re-enact the play, as if he was "Joltin' Joe." Folks laughed, except the guy who bet against the Yankees. The event was written on black board with white chalk dipped in a Dixie Cup of water, "DiMaggio-HHR-5th-1 on."

Men came from far and wide to shoot pool, right here in "river city....that's pool, capital P, capital O, capital O, capital L." Usually bet between themselves, competition was keen. Premier among them, "Statesboro" Crawford, good with a cue stick as anyone in the southland, could be found earning a few dollars, plying his trade. His games, "Nine Ball," attracted spectators and bettors. Walter "Stick" Howard, "Cool" Ruben Cooley, "Little" Lew Kooden, David "Rat" Shoob, also top shooters. Most afternoons one of them played some fellow who had little or no chance to win. "Stick" spotted a guy seven balls, all he had to do is make one to win, couldn't. Greats of Pooldom, Willie Mosconi, "Minnesota Fats," Willie Hoppe, Ralph Greenleaf, made the scene.

Here, celebrities, sports stars, dignitaries gathered to "see and be seen." Baseball greats who stopped in, Connie Mack, Casey Stengel, Joe DiMaggio, Charlie Keller, Bill Dickey, Joe Gordon, "Babe" Ruth, Ty Cobb, Dizzy Dean, Robin Roberts, Ralph Branca, Early Winn, Enos Slaughter, Warren Spahn, Johnny Sain; Football stars, Charlie Trippi, Sammy Baugh, Sid Luckman, "Bronco" Nagurski, Wally Butts, Bobby Dodd, Mal Cook; Golfers, Sammy Snead, Ben Hogan, Gene Sarazen, Hobart Manley; Famous song writer, "Savannah's Own," Johnny Mercer; Movie stars,

Charles Coburn, "Savannah's Own;" Clark Gable, Robert Mitchum, George Raft, as well as figures from the "underworld," Frank Costello, Meyer Lansky, "Bugsy" Siegel, Benny Gordon, Ben Levine, Frank Ericson, "World's biggest book maker." All had to put in appearances when in town.

Willie Mosconi. One of the five "Greatest Cueist of the Twentieth Century, according to *Billiard's Digest's People' Poll.*"

The Philadelphia, Pa., billiards prodigy began playing for stakes at age six, who, a year later challenged, but lost, to then World's Champion, Ralph Greenleaf. Willie's father owned a "pool hall" below the boy's bedroom, and at age five began playing while standing on a wood box, although his father tried to deny him access to the tables. Willie displayed a talent that his stunned father began showing the kid off in matches at his and other "pool halls." During the "great depression," he played for prize money, soon learning that tourney masters had an analytic sense of the game far superior to that of "pool hustlers," out to con inferior players. Fast, nervous style, won the World's Championship fifteen times and, at last crushed the real life "Minnesota Fats," before a world-wide audience on television's "Wide World of Sports." Probably the most well known pool player of all time; he honored the sport as it honored him in return.

In 1947, 1949 and 1951, "Bo Peep" invited Mosconi to put on a clinic and exhibition, play locals and other nationally known "shooters." Always a free show, the Champion packed them in 19 East Congress, was warmly received. Over one hundred stood in line to shake his hand. Prior to the exhibition, "Bo" stopped all activity in the room by turning off lights over each table, then in a loud, clear voice state, - "Gentlemen, I present to you, the greatest pool player that ever lived, the Champion of the World, Mister, Willie Mosconi!" Taking over, Willie introduced himself, spoke briefly about his back ground, history, how he got started, at the conclusion thereof, he stated, "Bo, I may not be the greatest that ever lived, but, I will do 'till he comes along!" The best dressed player to ever pick up a stick, he was suave, sophisticated, short, Italian, with a great personality and easy smile. Beginning with a few trick shots, one of which, he placed one ball in front of six pockets, and make them all with one shot. Then he moved immediately to demonstrate and explain the finer points of the game. A contest arranged, amid continuous chatter, cracking jokes, he thoroughly entertained the crowd. "O.K., you get one shot today, take advantage of it!" "Oh, my goodness, you didn't miss that, did you?" "Have a seat over there next to "Bo," and watch the master, you may actually learn something!" Mosconi displayed his ability by making 156 straight shots without missing, an incredible feat, not matched either before or after, in town. Ten and one-half racks, even the best Savannah players, and "Bookie, the rack boy," were impressed. That accomplishment will forever be remembered in sporting circles.

Willie Moscóni lived an exemplary life, he died in 1993 at the age of eighty years. God Bless! May he Rest in Peace.

The locals, too numerous to mention, made "Bo Peep's" their "hangout." Ruben Cooley, Bernie Kramer, Pete Palefsky, were his "Boys." They had a group of friends whom they met and remained close until the day they died. All enjoyed betting a few "bucks" on games, rooted fiercely for their teams. Cheering, clapping as they listened to the radio broadcast. Discussions between them, Bobby Hornstein, "Hank" Wiseman, and Charlie "Chuck" Grossman, as who was baseball's best pitcher, batter; became loud and animated, frequently concluded by saying, "You are crazy!" But, tomorrow was another day and they returned to begin anew. Charlie Grossman, premier masseur in the town's history, worked at Jewish Educational Alliance for years, "Made millions in oil, baby oil. Seen more fat than Oscar Meyer." Lovable, articulate, personable, prince among men.

Meyer freely put in his "two cents." "The town is full of guys, who think they're mighty wise!" Followed by loud, staccato laugh, that became his trademark. Willie "Stuffy" Ennis, clever, young, stylish, Irish clerk, sold punch board chances, tips, where you could win up to $50.00, and, kept supply of nickels available for pinball machines. Meyer's favorite joke, told on one boy he went with to buy a condom, asked for "size six and seven-eights." Making fun of customers was a pre-occupation, "He is too cheap, squeezes Lincoln so hard, he cries!"

"Coxie" Brind, only permanent, professional drunk that ever lived; sailed the seven seas, ninety days a year, remainder he got slobbering, staggering, wet your pants, drunk. "I can drink any man under the table." Liquor, Beer, Wine, Vanilla, Anti-freeze, anything alcohol was consumed. Led the St. Patrick's Day Parade a few years, his red nose, brighter than Rudolph's, glowing in the sun; waving, smiling at everyone, all along the parade route throwing kisses to ladies.

Murray "Killer" Rosen, a tough Brooklyn, N. Y., professional pugilist, practically lived at 19 East Congress Street. His claim to fame, "Shake the hand, that shook the hand of the great John L. Sullivan!" Willie Pep, Jimmy

Braddock, Carlos Chavez, Primo Carnera, were a few of the fighters who visited.

Throughout the year, Saturday was always big, important, interesting and fun at "The Finest in the South." Sporting gentry came in to see what was happening. If it was fall and football season, crowd assembled to read *"The Sporting News,"* scores, odds on games. Style show time, men from all walks of life, dressed in blue jeans and cotton shirts to imported silk suits. *Morris Levy's Men Shop*, on Broughton Street, across Congress Lane from "Bo Peep's." Stylists were Levy employees, including Morris Levy, himself; Henry Lehwald, Sr., Max Lipsey, Charlie Schwartz, all impeccably dressed in latest fashions; beautiful shirts, ties, suits and sport coats of only finest quality. "Clothes horse," Meyer referred to Lehwald. It was tradition for many of the patrons to stop in after synagogue, to show off their latest finery. "Best dressed category," included Julius Kaminsky, Jack Levy, "Izzy" Movsovitz, Meyer Tenenbaum, Hymie Godolphin. No telling who would appear, how long they'd stay, or what their interest. Certainly roast beef sandwich was an attraction. Atmosphere was unlike any other, "Absolutely incomparable," celebrated actor Charles Laughton often remarked in soft, English accent that endeared him to movie goers for years. "Really."

One really nice Savannah native that began shooting pool at an early age was Charlie Holm. He wore his first pair of long pants into the establishment in 1947, when a mere lad of sixteen. Long, tall, skinny Irish kid with freckles and piercing green eyes. Loved to shoot, acquired considerable skill at the master's hands, practiced several hours a day, after school. Quiet, unassuming, charming, ready smile. Well liked by all regulars, and "just crazy to play that game." He'd walk in, stand around, waiting to be invited to play. "Alright, thank you, name your game, a friendly little thing, maybe you can teach me something...always willing to learn." Eventually the contest proceeded to a small wager, and money proceeded from challenger's pocket to Charlie's.

A natural born politician, Mrs. Holm's little boy campaigned vigorously for G. Elliott Hagan in his successful bid for U. S. House of Representatives from First District of Georgia, including Savannah. He was rewarded by appointment to a responsible position with the Federal government in Washington, D. C. In fact, Charlie and "Bo's" second son actually saved the day for their candidate, when they rescued a ballot box from one county official, who took it home "for safe keepin'." They followed custodian home, knocked on front door at ten o'clock P.M., advised him through a closed door, that the second son was "a reporter from *Time Magazine*, to interview you, as to how and why you have the Official ballot box?" Of course, that was not exactly right, however, the box was immediately returned, and the two young men remained at that courthouse until morning, when they supervised authorized personnel obtain control of the same. "Thank you, very much Charlie and second son.

That particular election was "too close to call," so, you might say, these two young men made a major contribution to "clean politics," in their native State. Journalists from several major news organizations pursued the story, *The New York Times* published it on the front page. Elliott was quick to identify the "hero's," lavished praise over them, for "insight and integrity!"

Later, Charlie spearheaded "Bo" Ginn's victory for the same office, Ginn was Hagan's top assistant and worthy successor. Holm received another, more prestigious appointment in Washington; remained there following his career until retirement. Washington's gain was Savannah's lost. Isn't it funny that so many of Savannah's most talented young people left town to pursue their life's work? Many became highly successful and prominent in their chosen field. Pause, reflect, children from "old Savannah Families," :- Pano, Andris, Shoob, Silver, Rabhan, Holm, Odrezin, Dillon, McAlpin, Killorin, McGinn, Von Waldner, Flanigan, Mendel, Landers, Robbins, Flanders, Pacetti, Aliffi, Barnes, Griffin, Black, Greene, Whitman, Kelley, Spence, Thompson, Greer, on and on. Huge depository of talent, these unique individuals, men only, comprise a tiny segment of those who departed Chatham County in search of "greener pastures," which deprived that area of its most valuable resources. Who can explain it? Who can tell you why? Rich men attempt to reason, wise men never try! One can only hope that some day "leaders" will strive to correct this ancient malady. Too bad, Savannah!

One could devote an entire chapter about two of the boys. Walter "Stick" Howard, six feet tall, slim build, garnered him "Stick," as well as the fact that he could do more things with a cue ball than a monkey could do with a peanut. He arrived most days after his "regular job," to meet and talk the talk about whatever. Objective, to engage in a friendly little pool game, Eight Ball, Nine Ball, Snooker or Rotation. Pleasant, quiet talking, with an affable smile that was completely disarming, could talk anyone into playing, and make them feel as though they actually had a chance to win. Regal persona. Select a cue stick off the rack on wall, place it on table, roll it over several times to assure that it was balanced and straight, proper weight, usually 21 ounces. Few practice shots, little conversation, bet made, then a shot to end rail to determine who "breaks." Breaking was a huge advantage, especially to a good "stick man."

The break in Nine Ball usually avails shooter of one ball in a pocket, thus earning a second shot, continuing until shooter missed. Person making the Nine Ball wins the game. Average game lasts ten to fifteen minutes; with "Stick," it took half that. A shooting machine. His performance, if graded, had to be 98 out of a possible 100. Really made it look easy, as precise as brain surgery. Devoted considerable time teaching others the art of shooting in a patient relaxed manner.

More times than not, "Stick" pocketed a ball on the break, gaining an advantage over opponent. Before making that all important first shot, chalk cue; a small cube of hard blue chalk, indented on top, was carefully applied to cue stick, not unlike a woman applying lipstick, using care and precision. Chalk provides the tip with a slightly better "hold," helps eliminate slipping off cue ball when struck with considerable force, creating speed up to 90 miles per hour.

After winning, folded "green," placed it in left front shirt pocket, commenting, "You played good, better luck next time." Or, "I was lucky." Smile, not bragging, just a good old southern boy, doing his thing. One of "Bo's" favorite people.

Second individual, Lester "Statesboro" Crawford, also superior with cue stick. Big man, six foot six, steel worker by habit, "Shooter by choice." Blonde, curly hair that fell over his forehead when shooting, eagle eyes. Could he shoot? Does a shark poop in the sea? Truly professional, in every sense of the word. "I come to play, haven't had a game all week, and I'm ready for Freddie." Known all over, and that reputation was well earned. "Smart guys," from New York City, couldn't resist taking on "that country bumpkin…with a name like Statesboro." "Boro," exacted revenge on those "Yankee bastards," for indiscretions perpetrated during the war between the states. Forget? Hell NO! Many a " wise guy," received an expensive education at the hands of the "Boro." Vanquished, they left mumbling to themselves, "I must a' eat too much, next time he's mine, all mine." Yeah, Right!

These two men seldom played each other, simply out of respect. When they played, it was serious as a heart attack. They always got the "front table," which was maintained in immaculate condition, well lighted, thoroughly level from side to side, front to back. Whenever the "front table," was occupied, you knew damn well that you were watching the very best; men who performed superbly; spectators gathered quickly to witness the best free sport spectacle in Savannah.   It was obvious that they relished the opportunity, that they were proud, good, decent, hard working individuals. Kind of men that could most definitely be role models. Never a harsh or profane word, nor ill mannered, rude or discourteous. True southern gentlemen in the finest traditions of Dixieland, where I was born.

CHAPTER TWO

What was it that kept people coming to "Bo Peep's" over a span of twenty-six years? Him.

He loved people. He loved the "action." Demonstrated his concern for his fellow man by contributing to every church, synagogue or charity that ever came to see him. For many years he contributed large donations to Temple Mickve Israel, B. B. Jacob Synagogue, The Cathedral of St. John the Baptist, The Christ Church, Greek Orthodox Church, Benedictine Military School, St. Vincent's Academy, Jewish Educational Alliance, B'nai B'rith, Catholic Young People's Association, Salvation Army, Girl Scouts of America; before there was a United Way, there was "Bo Peep's."

Possessor of enormous empathy for people less fortunate than he. For over ten consecutive years, he fed one hundred fifty (150) needy people at his restaurant on Thanksgiving Day, and gave them baskets of food as they left. Standing at front door, shaking hands with every one who came through the line, smile on his face, pat on the back, good wishes for all. He fed the hungry, clothed the naked, helped hundreds of Savannahians.

Christmas, too, was a big day. Bonus for all employees, food, candy, toys for children. There never was a more generous, kind, caring person; before, or after, "Bo Peep." That name will live forever in the hearts and minds of those he helped. It is mentioned in conversation by people who personally did not know him, but had heard of him. Whenever people remember "the old days," that name is recalled, time and time again.

49

One question frequently asked about this "little man," "Where does he get that persistent drive, energy, will or desire?" The answer: "Determination to succeed, overcome handicaps; improve his condition and that of his family; to give them more and better than he received, not only his wife, four children; but also brother, sisters, nephews, nieces, in-laws. Money, because it was the mark of success, by which he thought others evaluated him."

An average day began at 7:00 A.M., bath, dress casually, reserving a neck tie for special occasions; collect papers, records; breakfast of *Wheaties,* tea or coffee; walk to corner of Washington Avenue and Abercorn Street, to catch a bus, or, if in a hurry, as usually the case, call his favorite *Yellow Cab,* and stand out front of his house located at 119 Washington Avenue, until it arrived.

Upon arrival, commenced checking with "Tiger," Joe McCabe at the hotel, John Jackson, Chef and Chief Cook; return telephone calls, go to his "private office," assemble bets, notes, memos. Always busy, always active, always in motion. Estimated that he walked over one mile a day, just in the enterprise. Although he probably did not read Robert Louis Stevenson, he epitomized a passage from "El Dorado," – "To travel hopefully is a better thing than to arrive, and the true success is to labour."

Honest, kind, earned a little, spent a little less, to make on the whole a family happier for his presence; renounce when necessary, but not be embittered; to keep a few close friends and grapple them to his soul with hoops of steel; and, remain friends with himself.

Politicians absolutely fascinated him. One favorite saying, "How can a man spend $250,000.00 for a job paying $25,000.00?" That made good sense then, it makes better sense now. He met all of the politicians of his time;

city, county, state, federal. They flocked to his door seeking donations, which, at that time was in "cash." No receipts, records, really convenient for "politicos," as they took money, and in some cases, "bit the hand that fed them." Then, too, these guys had unmitigated gall to call themselves "good Christians, and do- gooders." Funny, isn't it, they talked about all the "good" things they would do, if elected, and they "will clean up Savannah!" Test of time reveals they should have started with themselves, clean up their minds, morals, lives and conduct. Most of "the do-gooders needed to get out a broom and sweep streets, they and Savannah would profit." "Bo" understood their little games and charades, what he didn't understand was their avarice, greed and hatred. America was founded by good men, who honestly believed that service to the country was an honor, privilege, highest calling of man. Many of Savannah's "reformers" had no idea about those high principles, their only concern was themselves, and how they could line their pockets, at others expense, being "land grabbers." "The Petty Politicians."

It is the essence of responsibility to place the public good ahead of personal gain. Most politicians do their best, and in the modest, un- spectacular, decent way; which, of course is highest form of public service. However, every day in a shameful variety of ways, selfish actions of a small minority sully the honor of the city. It was this conduct by the "reformers," that "Bo" could not tolerate and refused to deal.

A little known historical fact is that "Bo" was a major financial and political supporter of three consecutive Georgia Governors.

Richard B. Russell, Jr., while campaigning for office in 1931, came to Savannah seeking support, and, like a heat seeking missile, targeted Congress Street, under guidance of Sol Kaminsky, Harry Berman, Mc Rae, Georgia; and Dr. Abe Tenenbaum of Augusta, Ga.

"Bo," it's important that you get to know our next Governor. He needs you, and you may possibly need him one day," said Sol, who knew that "Bo" possessed the first, newest, prettiest and biggest convertible automobile in town, having just sold it to him. Such a vehicle would be "just ideal to campaign, and make speeches from." This car was photographed by Georgia newspapers and circulated repeatedly all over the state, Russell standing in rear, speaking to a large crowd. The four man group was seated in the front of the restaurant, enjoyed a hearty meal, drinks, fellowship, as twenty to thirty men came to meet Russell, and make $20.00 contributions. Russell was elected and began his tenure as Governor on June 27, 1931. He became one of Georgia's most able and respected Chief Executives, and continued his illustrious career as United States Senator, where he achieved great distinction and honor. The United States Courthouse in Atlanta was dedicated, "The Richard B. Russell Building," a bronze likeness placed at the front entrance. It was primarily due to Russell's influence as Chairman of Armed Services Committee, that the state obtained numerous federal projects and training facilities for Army, Navy, Coast Guard, Air Force. Savannah, Hinesville, Bainbridge, Atlanta, Columbus, Macon and Augusta, all benefited therefrom.

Early in 1932 Eugene Talmadge made it known that he was running for Governor, like Russell before him, hailed from a small town in Georgia, faced with a major obstacle of raising campaign funds. Of course, who better to turn to than Sol Kaminsky and his pal Harry Berman, both of whom, by this time, where well known in political circles. Sol having become Savannah's outstanding new car salesman, owner of a Cadillac agency, named "Chatham Motors." Berman, from Mc Rae, a long time friend and neighbor of the Talmadge family, owned and operated a department store named "Berman's." It was like "déjà vu, all over again." Those three could unquestionably sell large loads of ice to Eskimos, "Bo," resembled "putty in their hands." Supplied them with food, drinks and lodging at "*The De Soto Hotel,*" also, a "barbecue" for three hundred people on Victory Drive near Skidaway Road intersection; as well as use of his now famous convertible, with driver. 'Gene first used the expression at this "barbecue," "People in Georgia, from Rabun Gap to Tybee light are supportin' Eugene Talmadge for Governor!" After it was over, 'Gene summed it up, "Bo, if everybody who ate my barbecue, votes for me, I won't have any trouble being elected!" He was right!

At parting he reminded his three benefactors, "You are fine fellows, salt of the earth, I will never forget you three as this is the help I needed to get my campaign up and running; I'll never forget you, and I want you to know the door to the Governor's Office is always open to you." He was elected, assumed office on January 10, 1933, served four years. Sol made sure he kept his promise, he sold numerous cars to Georgia State Patrol, with "the damndest, biggest blue light and siren anyone ever saw." How about that? Eugene Talmadge was the consummate politician. A "helluvah speaker, fire brand," relentless campaigner. Dressed in a white shirt, red "galluses" or suspenders, cotton pants, black shoes, black horn rimmed eye glasses; he made one unbeatable candidate in Georgia. Blessed with ability not only to say what he thought, but also say what the people wanted to hear, the way they wanted to hear it, delivered in a booming voice, hand pumping, finger pointing manner. Never met a stranger, knew necessary hand shakes, quick witted, talked with that south Georgia twang, could party with the best of them. Enjoyed a touch of bourbon, every now and then.

At the barbecue he raised over $1,900.00 in cash, $1,500.00 in checks, which was considered excellent. People stood in line to "press the flesh," and give him $20.00 bills, while patting him on the back and shouting, "Give 'em Hell, Gene!" "I will tell the truth, and he will think it's Hell!" One famous utterance, "I may surprise you, but I will not deceive you!" The Talmadge name was like magic, Eugene's son, Herman Eugene Talmadge was also elected Governor, and followed that by being elected United States Senator, where he became a well respected, distinguished member, highlighted by his outstanding service on the historic "Water Gate Commission."

A statue, over twelve feet tall adorns the State Capitol grounds in Atlanta, illustrating 'ol 'Gene pointing his index finger as he did frequently, when making an emphatic point.

May he Rest in Peace.

The third consecutive, unique candidate was E. D. Rivers, who was elected Governor, served from January 12, 1937 to 1941. He came in "Bo Peeps," un-announced, without introduction, in a most matter-of-fact, business like manner, "You were such a big help to Talmadge, I trust you will consider my candidacy. Education is the keynote of my campaign, I earnestly solicit your support, and I hope you will join." He could not have hit a more responsive vein in the "little man," who well knew the value of education, or, the lack thereof. Responded immediately, assuring Rivers that he'd receive every consideration, but, because of the very unusual position that he now found himself in, could not be as visible as in Talmadge's race, Contacting Shelby Myrick, Sr., John J. Bouhan, Joseph A. Mendel, Emanuel Lewis, and two others whom he regarded as "well informed and tuned-in to the political scene." Concluded that Rivers could be elected, and surely wanted to be with the winner, again. Raising money "was no big deal," as liquor dealers, beer distributors, bar owners, coin machine operators were anxious to contribute to such a "worthy cause." Several brought checks in various amounts from $1,000.00 to $2,500.00. Rivers was contacted personally, returned to Savannah "post haste," to pick up his funds. He was obviously impressed, teary eyed, as he kissed "Bo" on the left cheek, saying, "This is the largest contribution I've received; thank you, thank you, thank you. May God bless you and your family."

In early 1940's, long before Martin Luther King, Jr., addressed equal employment, "Bo Peep" hired blacks in his businesses when few others gave them any consideration. Some questioned him, "Why you?" His response, "Why not me?" Compassionate, caring, considerate of his fellow man. Completely unbiased; color blind. Coming from "poor people" himself, understood problems and plight of those less fortunate than he. He knew what it was like to be poor, and, a member of a minority. Counseled not only his wife and children, but also employees, to "treat every body the way you want to be treated." Those "blacks" became good, trusted, long time employees. Every member of their families knew and loved "Mr. Bo Peep." No one could speak ill of him in their presence. He'd been "tried and found not wanting." They brought friends, relatives, even "preachers," to meet this "good man."

On a "one on one situation," no person that ever lived in Savannah, Georgia, did more good for more people than he. NO BODY. The good Samaritan, fed the hungry, clothed the naked, rendered aid to the sick, employed the handicapped. He soothed the grieved, never shunned the sorrowful, nor the wretch undone; most positively unlike the hard, selfish and the proud. Treated "paupers and kings," the same; "a maxim often tried, right was right, and there he would abide." Applied this rule without exception, always unheralded, never expecting anything in return. A good man.

He married a beautiful Catholic girl from one of Savannah's largest families, when "she was just a kid." Seven years younger, he in his mid-twenties. Together, they had four children, three boys and a girl. All four attended college, two sons graduated, one with an LL.B from the University of Georgia School of Law; the other with an M. D. from the University of Georgia School of Medicine. Both of whose accomplishments are deserving of books in their name, but are not the subject of this one. The marriage vows were solemnly kept until his death. People say "opposites attract." That could not be more true in this instance. He, flamboyant, public, easy, outgoing, impatient. She, quiet, that is until you got "her Irish up;" private, personal, family oriented. A loving Mother whose life centered only on family interests, and, what is best for her children. Good homemaker, excellent cook, spotless house keeper. It did not matter how large the house, it simply had to be spic and span. Her home was her castle, and friends of the children were always welcome and warmly received. She did all grocery shopping at *Smith Brothers Market* on Habersham Street, where she knew everybody, and everybody knew her, greeting her in their inimitable, kind, friendly manner; "Good morning, Mrs. Silver, can I help you?" Seeing to it that vegetables, meats, poultry, were only the freshest, highest quality in town. In return, "those Smith Brothers," were recommended without hesitation, "They are the nicest people to deal with, I've ever seen."

What was his home life like?

He was first, last, always a "family man." Loved his children more than life itself. Worked hard for his money, upon returning home, was quiet, affable, easy-going. An authoritative person, spoke in a modest tone, using hands for emphasis. A referee, didn't have much choice, because the children saved all of their arguments, or feuds, for the moment they saw him. Sometimes the matter was settled before his involvement, as one threatened the other, "If you don't do that, I'll tell Daddy as soon as he gets home." Many times the wife used the same threat. His word was unquestionably final. Never resorted to physical abuse, no hits, slaps or knocks. Usually admonished in firm tone, "Do not fight between yourselves." All four children called him "Daddy." Wife called him "Bo Peep" when talking about him, outside of the family; but "Honey," to his face. Did all in his power to move into good neighborhoods, constantly striving to improve their status. Children attended the best schools in town.

A great story teller, had numerous tales to relate. Friends, relatives, employees, customers were "fair game." When the second son won a case, or subject of an article in the *Savannah Morning News,* he carried it around in his coat pocket, to make sure no one missed reading it; some times stopping strangers on the street to show it to them. "That's my boy!"

As public as he was, absolutely insisted on privacy in his home life. Keeping long hours, incessant telephone calls, meetings, constant stream of men coming in and out of the business, was incredibly tiring on him. It was a rare treat, usually Sunday, he could "take a break," and when it came, he reveled in it. Home was special, immediate family, his pride and joy. Whole purpose was to do good for them, that they would not have to endure the extreme hardships and deprivation that he experienced. Competitive by nature, it extended to his sons. Every effort was made to see that they grew up in a normal household, participate in sports. Baseball bats, gloves, balls, were presented them as soon as they got old enough to run. Footballs, helmets, shoulder pads, uniforms, came with season's change. Complete set of *McGregor Master Tourney* golf clubs in leather bag were given to second son at age fifteen. In the attic of home was a Championship Regulation Pool Table complete with ivory balls, ten pool sticks, all related accessories.

First family in his neighborhood to acquire a large television, watched every sports program possible, loved having sons watch with him. A most memorable experience immediately recalled was the game in Green Bay, Wisconsin, between Green Bay "Packers," and Baltimore "Colts," on the "frozen tundra." He picked the "Packers," invited the second and third son to bet $10.00 on the game. Every play was diagnosed to the nth degree, and each invited to contribute his "two cents," to discussion. Make it clear.

There they sat, yelling and screaming at the television screen as though they were there in person. At conclusion, bets were paid to the winner.

Another family outing was visit Grayson Stadium on East Victory Drive, to watch the Savannah "Indians" play the Jacksonville "Tars" in the old South Atlantic Baseball League. ("Sally" League.) That game in particular is easy to recall because it was the first game that Henry Aaron played in Georgia. The "Hammer," as he was called later in his career, had a most unique "wiggle," when stepping into the batter's box.

"Daddy," was the children's choice. Time flew when they were with him, and he was attentive to their needs. Interested in their lives, unrivaled protector, loving, caring to each, but reserving a special adoration of the youngest child, his daughter, whom he called, "little lady."

Generous to a fault, he purchased each child an automobile when they attained sixteen years of age. Personally taught them to drive, which in a few cases stopped short of mayhem. That initial lesson, usually on Skidaway Road (dirt) was a test of "Job's patience." How many times that car started with a lurch, stopped in a jerk, was unbelievable. Immediately upon return home, the whole family was summoned, description given, amidst laughter, culminating with, "I'm sure we will do better next time." Then privately tell the Mother, "I sure hope so, I don't know how much more of this I can stand. We ran off the road three times, and almost in a ditch once. God!"

It is amusing how much you can recall, once photographs are viewed, notes and letters read; so many incredible incidents remembered. Photography was a love. Purchased almost every camera that came to market, from the original "box type," to latest in movie cameras. Hundreds of photographs and movie reels were taken of his children, family and friends. Movies were shown on a portable, roll up screen, he, the narrator. Names, dates, locations carefully recorded on the yellow carton that enclosed *Kodak Film.* On occasion, due to "error beyond control," heads were cut off, causing him to laugh out loud 'till he got tears in his eyes, trying to determine "who that guy is?" Many of the movies are priceless today as they depict Savannah as it was in 1930's and 40's. Broughton Street parades, stock car races when the "Flocks" were kings, Benedictine events, and various activities at the "Big Park."

That was his way of showing his children how much he loved them, the extent of interest in everything they did, whenever, where ever. "Father's love," was all consuming, limitless, continuous, warm, personal, passionate. This indelible impression became engraved on their collective memories and consciences. Each was infinitely better off as a result of knowing him.

He hired, or did business with, all of his in-laws, at least fifteen in number, did it willfully and cheerfully. All they had to do was ask, he found a way.

Sunday was his day at home. A day or rest, relaxation, time for family, and, as such, he insisted that every Sunday at 1:00 P.M. "dinner" be served in the dining room, it being mandatory that all members be dressed, present, prompt. Nothing, nor no one, could interfere with tradition. Frequently a guest or two, "broke bread," if the dining table was inadequate, then, the two youngest were tactfully moved to the breakfast room. Usually eight people were seated at a dark mahogany antique table with arm chairs at each end, reserved for "Mama and Daddy." Dinners served, more often than not, fried chicken, rice, gravy, green beans, corn, sweet iced tea, and a special treat, home made, hand churned ice cream. Second favorite, prime tenderloin of roast beef, creamy mashed potatoes, brown gravy or au jus; mixed green salad, beets. "Mama" was chief cook, in her exclusive domain, whose culinary feats were legendary. Her "Fruit Cake," was like nectar from the Gods. Something she made twenty- five pounds, every Christmas, dousing each two and one-half pound portion in "bourbon" whisky, then wrapped it in brown waxed paper surrounded by aluminum foil, distributed to family far and wide.

At completion of the meal, conversation was encouraged on any subject matter from Bach to baseball, adolescence to zoo, school or career. When the children were young, Sunday drive to somewhere, Tybee, generally; Beaufort, Georgetown, Bluffton, South Carolina. Stop en-route for ice cream, fudge, cold drinks. The patriarch had a "purple passion," for ice cream, preferably "home made." You know, only good stuff, fresh cream, sugar, vanilla or chocolate. It was not unusual to load the family car, drive thirty miles to get some "I scream, you scream, we all scream for ice cream." Memorable gems.

Summer time at Savannah Beach, Tybee Island, was a high point in his year. In 1938, having purchased the last vacant lot on Shirley Road, five lots from the ocean and next to Harrell "Savannah Lumber Co." Murray; retained Cy Span to draw plans for a residence. It was his certain mission to personally construct that house. Upon completion of plans, a mason, carpenter, and electrician were hired to assist. Make no mistake about it, he, and he alone, was going to supervise construction from digging foundation, to raising the roof. Only finest materials were obtained, labor commenced in January, completion date of June 1. Every thing went well until time came to paint the wall of the "sleeping porch," designated for his children. The painter, a close personal friend, thought to be reliable.

What was unknown, his love of the "brown" bottle. Alcoholic is putting it mild. "I can complete this job in two days, if you give me complete control, without interference." "O.K. my friend, you got it. I'll return Saturday afternoon for inspection."

In anxious anticipation, bounding up stairs to second level, proclaiming loudly, "coming ready or not," the "little man" was greeted, ushered into the area. Looked good, touching the wall carefully, detected that it was "sticky." What is the matter?" "Oh, nothing, it will be dry before nightfall." "Alright, thank you."

Following day, "move in day." Three truck loads of newly purchased furniture was delivered, one man made an error of leaning against the wall. His shirt stuck securely, as he attempted to pull away, it tore from top to bottom, hanging like a drapery. Cursing to the top of his lungs; "Bo" rushed to see cause, was appalled at the sight. Nothing quite like a newly painted wall with cotton shirt affixed.

"Man, I got to call that painter. I'll be damned if I can figure out what is the matter here." Rushing to town, painter was contacted, seemed to be under the influence, as he was unable to speak coherently. Slamming down the phone, "Bo" returned to Tybee to consult A. P. Solomon, a contractor, to determine cause of "sticky" condition. "Good lord, the painter did not properly mix in thinner." Search produced empty thinner cans, whereupon the painter's helper stated, "John drank the thinner."

Ten years later, that wall remained "sticky to the touch." Providing a permanent joke in the family. Painter died an early death, occasioned by liver problems. His wife said, "John couldn't resist any thing containing alcohol."

Other than that minor inconvenience, the well built house has survived several major hurricanes without damage, still stands in all it's splendor.

In those days, Beach community comprised leadership of Chatham County. John A. Peters, Sr., Dr. J. Reid Broderick, Sol Kaminsky, J. Harold "Georgia Supply" Mulherin; B. I. Friedman, founder and owner of Friedman's Jewelers, Inc.; Frank C. Mathews, fish purveyor; Dan Sheehan, Plate Glass Co; Basil Morris, Attorney; Joseph F. Griffin, fuel oil; Mrs. S. Eichholz, Real Estate tycoon; Fred "Camp SABECA" Garris; A. F. Solms, Hotel owner; Merritt W. Dixon, Mrs. Lilly Bell Gann, teacher and restaurant owner. All, summer time residents, in what was then, a small, white settlement.

An early to bed, early to rise believer, "Bo" jogged one mile on the beach, to the Tybee Pavilion, took a breather, returned home in less than twenty minutes; long before jogging became popular.

Surf fishing at Tybee was a memorable experience. First, as an annual ritual, he proceeded to Stubbs Sporting Goods on W. Congress Street, where he talked with the owner to obtain vital recommendations for "fishing equipment." Amicably obliging, the gentlemen suggested an eight foot imported bamboo fishing rod; stainless steel, rust proof, level winding reel; six hundred feet of finest fishing line; scoop net; shrimp net; pliers, wicker fish basket, "to hold your catches;" six different kinds and size hooks; six lead sinkers, fish stringer, white "African Safari" brimmed hat; dark glasses, sun screen, "skeeter" repellant, and vest. Fishing was serious business.

Surf fishing was extremely difficult and unrewarding. For a novice like "Bo" it was impossible, but, hey, that didn't matter in the least bit.

Sunday afternoon, over sand dunes, through "sea oats," to the ocean he trod to his appointed destination, wind whipping through his curly hair, determined look on face, approached ocean's edge, ready to engage fish of any species. Using frozen shrimp as bait, he cast a mighty cast, thirty feet out from where he stood in ankle deep water. Nothing. Another cast, nothing. Three straight casts that created "back lash," tangling the line, necessitating fifteen minutes untangling time. Four more casts resulting in lost bait, and analysis, "damn crabs," Well, at least the fish were being fed. By this time several neighbors ventured forth with suggestions, including consensus, "this is the wrong time, and wrong place; they don't bite here." All, well intentioned but placidly ignored; "What do they know?"

After all, persistence and determination was the fabric of his life. An hour passed, all efforts were doomed. "Maybe next week, maybe the moon ain't right."

Next week, and two following weeks expired without success.

Then, on a Sunday afternoon, late August, the improbable happened! He actually hooked a poor, unsuspecting, tiny little "Whiting." With a hoop and a holler he started running backward out of the ocean, while winding line, and, of all unexpected, impossible events to occur, actually fell down flat on his back; struggling to his feet, continued excitedly, speedy withdrawal; approaching water's edge, fell again, this time dropping rod and reel. Panic set in, nervous anxiety turned to grief, as he picked himself up, continued running up the beach, until he fell the third time. David S. Bracker, champion fisherman, rushed to aid, "Are you hurt?" "Hell no, just go get that damn fish off the hook." Returning with catch, Dave observed, "It's about six inches!" "It can't be, I thought it weighed a pound." Spectators including Charlie Holm and "Dede" Mathews could not stop laughing, as they observed torn bathing trunks, fishing hat floating out to sea. "Well, there is always a next time."

In the mean while, fish slept soundly, because the "threat" had subsided.

That didn't quench his thirst for fishing, tried several more weeks that summer, learning as he went, explaining to his son, "Be careful, don't get excited, and for God's sake, don't run backward out of the water should you hook something!"

Another pleasure was setting up a powerful telescope on the breezy front porch to search horizon for ships and "submarines." "Oh?" "Yes, indeed!" On a pleasant Sunday afternoon while relaxing, World War, II, raging, a major calamity arose when he yelled, "Oh, my God, I see a German submarine! Call the Coast Guard, get the Chief of Police; the Commanding Officer at Fort Screven!" Rushing to his side, the second son shouting, "Let me see," knocked the telescope over, was severely chastised. In less than twenty minutes, Shirley Road was filled with Army, Navy and Coast Guard vehicles, all descending on his residence. Ranking officer demanded to see the "Nazi Sub," was amazed when some object resembling a submarine appeared. No body knew anything about this vessel, Coast Guard "Cutters" were dispatched without delay. Thirty to forty men assembled on the beach behind sand dunes, set up observation post. Eventually, aerial inspection was conducted by aircraft from Jacksonville Naval Air Station, reporting back, they had observed "an un-identified submarine." "Bo" immediately raised an American Flag on his permanent, concrete based, forty foot high flag pole; exclaiming, "Let's call the President!" "No, we must check with superior officers before any action, and we sure as Hell, cannot tell the newspaper." Four hours later, dark approaching, officer in charge stated, "This is top secret, we cannot make reference to this matter, whatsoever. The security of our country may be at stake." True story! Although it was discussed privately, it was not publicly acknowledged by government; but that did not matter, after all, we had seen it with our very own eyes!

Approximately two weeks later, the Commanding Officer, Naval Air Station, Jacksonville, Florida, visited "Bo" and two neighbors, who also had seen the "submarine," at Tybee Island. After a short questioning, in presence of two subordinates, Officer suggested the matter "be completely dismissed from your minds, for the best of all concerned, as this was a national security matter, and we really do not want to alarm anyone unnecessarily." He did not verify sighting, or results of extensive aerial surveillance. Needless to say, this, "keep it quiet," approach by government caused considerable apprehension among those who had seen the "submarine." One of whom stated emphatically, "I don't understand, if we are in jeopardy, why shouldn't people be told?"

Conversation changed direction, when, without pausing, the Officer asked, "Have any of you seen evidence of, or personally observe small boats or ships leaving the vicinity and sailing out beyond the four mile reef?" "Well, not directly," stated neighbor Bart, "but I have heard that it is being done on a regular basis; leaving early morning about five o'clock, returning evenings before dark, and, that two of them are shrimp boats." "Do you mean regular shrimp boats, rigged with nets?" "Yes, that is my understanding."

Officer requested that he report any other information he may receive on the subject to his subordinate. Then, followed with, "We believe local fisherman are supplying food, water, gasoline to our enemies. We look upon this as being very serious, in fact treason. Your help is earnestly solicited." "Treason?" "Damn right, treason!" Laughing, "Bo," suggested, "Hell, we can use my telescope, it's perfect, has a very long range, and incidentally, it's German. I invite neighbors and their families to take part, participate as much as they desire." "Excellent!"

"We do not have to watch all day, just during hours reported to me. My kid will jump at the opportunity." "Keep a pad nearby to record any sightings, time, date, direction they seem to move. Then, communicate that to us, when you feel it's becoming a pattern," the Lieutenant said quietly.

Several sightings were observed, and dutifully reported. Subsequent thereto, "Bo," was notified that two shrimp boats had, in fact, been seized. However, it seemed odd that the confiscations went un-reported in the local gazettes, *Savannah Morning News,* or, *Evening Press.* Regardless, as per the usual custom in small southern towns, news gets out. Sol Kaminsky heard from a friend in the U. S. Marshal's office; that three members of local families were arrested for participation in that nefarious scheme; shrimp boats seized, and federal indictments were being considered by the U. S. Attorney's Office in Savannah. All three participants were either of Italian or German heritage, or both. It was the topic of conversation at Tybee for weeks, as everyone got caught up in guessing game, "Who is it?" "Do I know them?" "Why isn't it public information?" A lawyer retained to represent one of the men, while in a drunken stupor, babbled name of one "suspect," knocking the socks off listeners, shocking several; he, interestingly enough from one of the more prominent families in Savannah. The culprits reason, clearly stated, "Blood is thicker than water!"

It is peculiar that some people actually felt that way during the "great war to end all wars." Some merely did it for love of the almighty dollar, others because they did not care less who won the war. Simply speaking, it mattered not, but, yet, this country was the haven they fled to in time of trouble or oppression. Interestingly, enough, a country wherein they prospered. These were not poor, ignorant misfits; these men were prominent, well-to- do, "moneyed," "church-going," local families that remain prominent even today, 2000 A.D. At the first opportunity they demonstrated their true colors. Not one member of any of these families served in the armed forces. Cowards, traitors, scum bags all! As Howard Cosell would say, "How about that, sports fans?" It is too disgusting seeing their filthy names in print.

Compare that to the fact "Bo Peep's" three sons all served honorably in the armed forces; one in U.S. Air Force, two in U.S. Navy, plus, three nephews, four brothers-in-law. If you were male, physically able, of age, then it was expected that "you do your duty, serve your country." That was the very least you could do. After all is said and done, to he who much is given, much is expected in return. May it always be so.

For weeks thereafter, this matter was cussed, discussed, pondered, dissected, resurrected, never reaching a reasonable, satisfactory conclusion; giving rise to much impatience, disgust, disappointment. "I cannot, for the life of me, bring myself to under- stand this disgraceful, irrational conduct. Let this be a good lesson to you, my children."

He did not drink, except, an occasional "schnapps" before dinner. However he maintained several leading brands of bourbon, scotch, vodka, fine wines, at home for guests.

Possessor of a "sharp tongue," generally left it outside. Preferring to contribute harmoniously in family circles.

Vacations longer than two days were rare, when he took one, the whole family went along; example, an automobile trip to New York City for 1939 World's Fair; packed wife, her youngest sister Anne, who lived with the family; three children, in a six passenger Cadillac Sedan automobile.

A real "workaholic," carried work home, staying up until 10:00 P.M., reviewing notes, scribbles, un-identified telephone numbers on numerous paper slips.

It was unique and somewhat strange, that the father was so well known, from earliest years children were curious, asking "Who?" "What?" "Where?" "When?" Minors were not permitted in "Bo Peep's Pool Room," however, that did not quench desire and curiosity, it was, of course, something to see, do or talk about.

A man of great emotion, easily touched, moved to point of tears whenever separation from his children, for more than three days, occurred. He hated to say, "Good bye." Eyes became tear filled, as he placed tongue in right cheek, grasping them in a bear hug; turn away. Never wanting loved ones to see him cry.

"Big men don't cry!"

"Oh, yes they do!"

CHAPTER THREE

One fine Spring day in 1934, when Azaleas were in bloom: - "Bo Peep, you got a long distance telephone call from somebody named John Roxborough." Meyer poked Willie Ennis in the ribs asking, "Who in Hell is John Roxborough?" "I dunno, sounds like a Yankee used car salesman."

"Hello, John, where you been, haven't heard from you in a few, since you played basketball, what can I do for you?" "You doing what? Managing who? Why you want to get in that racket, that's a tough game, and you don't know nothin' about it. Hired a trainer? Really? Well, I wish you all the best, let me hear from you as how it goes. Good luck!"

"Boss, you got us wonderin' who dat?"

"Old acquaintance, nothin' much to talk about, but, I will watch and let you know if anything comes from it." It certainly was not unusual for "Bo" to receive long distance calls from all over the world; trainers, managers, players, coaches, gamblers, you name it, he talked to them all.

That night, he could not help but wonder out loud, who is Joseph Louis Barrow? For sure, he didn't know, and did not know any one who knew. Following day, asked Murray "Killer" Rosen, all he got in return was a very quizzical expression on a rather blank face.

Few weeks passed, "Killer," while reading *The Ring Magazine,"* "The bible of boxing," in his Brooklyn accent proclaimed, "Joseph Louis Barrow is a black heavyweight, born in Lafayette, Alabama, twenty years ago, son of an Alabama sharecropper! Listen to this! He's been fighting amateur, and doin' pretty good, got a manager named John

70

Roxborough, from Detroit, Michigan; a former basketball player."

"Now you got my attention. Let me see that, I know John Roxborough, talked to him a few weeks ago, and have taken some of his lay off bettin' action in the past. He built quite a gambling business and attracts money like a magnet attracts metal; member of a very prominent Detroit family. Doesn't know diddley about the boxing racket, but it says here, he hired Jack "Chappy" Blackburn as trainer, that ain't no bad move."

"What kinda fight name is Joseph Louis Barrow? Sounds like a north Georgia lawyer, I heard of Barrow County, Georgia."

"Says here, and this is funny, when the guy filled out forms for an amateur fight, he didn't have enough room for his last name, so he began fighting under the name of Joe Louis. What a story! Now, you have the rest of the story!"

"Joe Louis," turned pro in 1934 and won the World Heavyweight Championship from James J. Braddock on June 22, 1937, by an eighth round knock out. (Provided by *The Ring Record Book.*) Louis was the "underdog," and John Roxborough telephoned "Bo" to take all action he could get, and, if it was too much on "the white guy," he would handle it. "Bo" took all bets. Sure was pleased with outcome. "John, you sure know how to pick 'em! Your push gave me confidence."

"Bo" traveled to see Joe Louis fight on two occasions, and was introduced to the Champ by Roxborough. He also met Nat Fleischer, publisher of *The Ring Magazine,* who described Louis' punching ability as follows: "He possesses an excellent jab, with real power in both hands. His right cross was as devastating as his left hook. His punches are so compact that I, and several others, believe that a Louis punch need only travel six inches to render an opponent unconscious. Honest to God!" "Bo's" impression, excellent. "Louis used his words as he did hid punches, comfortable, economy of effort, saying things in a way we all wish we had. Humble but proud!"

Several months elapsed, on April 1, 1938, Joe Louis was to defend his World Championship against Harry Thomas in Chicago, Illinois. The day of the fight "Bo" received a call from Roxborough, who told him to bet on Louis, and, as an additional wager, pick round five as the round Joe Louis will K. O. him. That's pretty good tip or information coming from the man's manager, so, certainly it had to be respected. "O. K., I'll take all action on Thomas, and call New York to Frank Ericson, bet him on Louis, and also pick round five."

It just so happens that one of Savannah's most colorful figures and all around good guy was present at that time, within hearing distance of the conversation. At conclusion Johnny Rovolis, a close friend, asked, "Bo, what's that all about?" Taking Johnny by the arm, they walked outside, and "Bo" whispered the information he just received. Rovolis, seeing great value in that "tip" said, "Get me down for Five Hundred on Louis, taking round five." "O. K., you got it!" That night, twenty patrons gathered to listen to national broadcast of the fight, blow by blow, and, surprise, surprise, Joe Louis knocked Thomas out in the Fifth Round! "Wow, can you beat that?"

Roxborough remained Louis' manager until World War, II, when, in 1942 Joe Louis enlisted as a Private in the United States Army, earning Twenty-one Dollars ($21.00) per month.

His life time record was seventy-one wins, three losses, and, was the Heavyweight Champion of the World from

June 22, 1937 until June 25, 1948; successfully defending his title twenty-five times. (Statistical information obtained from *The Detroit News.*)

Plagued with bad financial advice, Louis' lost almost all of the millions earned fighting. Moved to Las Vegas, Nevada, where he was employed for several years as "door man" at *Caesar's Palace.*

He died April 12, 1981 in Las Vegas.

"May he Rest in Peace."

Another incredible, unforgettable event occurred in "Bo Peep's" in October, 1938, after the World Series, in which the New York Yankees swept the Chicago Cubs four straight games by a combined score of 22 – 9. Yankee pitching that year was outstanding, compiling a 3.91 earned run average, establishing a record which remains today, due in large part to "Red" Ruffing, 21 – 7; "Lefty" Gomez, 18 – 12; "old Georgia boy," "Spud" Chandler; and Monte Pearson.

About 1:30 P.M. on Saturday, a rather shy, quiet, young man came in and approached the cash register over which Meyer presided. Several faithful were in attendance and seated nearby, two of whom recognized the individual immediately, poking each other, whispering, "You know who that is... "Yes, oh my God!" "Shhh, don't say nothin'."

"Sir, may I see Mr. Bo Peep? A friend of mine, "Spud" Chandler asked me to drop in to see him when I was in town."

"Well, he ain't here right now, but when he comes in, who should I say is waitin' to see him?"

The visitor, appearing a little surprised and somewhat bemused, quietly said, "I don't know if I can tell just anybody, who's calling, unless, of course, I know who it is that I am speaking to..."

By now, "Tiger," had almost swallowed his cigar, but determined to go along with the proceedings, keeping his head down over his check book pretending he was immersed in heavy duty book keeping.

"Ruben," stood up, moved closer to cigar display case to better hear the repartee, eyes glowing, hand over mouth. "Bubber' Johnson also intrigued with goin' ons, unloosened his tie and re-lit his cigar.

"Frego," stood next to him, "I can't miss this!" "Gully, come over."

"Well, this is a business, not a play ground, and we don't got time for games. If you want to see Mr. Bo Peep, then you got to go thru me, because, only me knows when he'll be in."

"Stuffy" Ennis left his punch board stand, to look around for the "little man." Locating him in his office in the rear, asked please come forward to avert disaster. Returning about half-way, they stopped suddenly, "I'd know that face anywhere, what's going on...? Wait, let's watch. Don't say anything."

Few more regulars came in, Julius "The Champ" Kaminsky; Melvin "The King" Karp, both automotive entrepreneurs; Sidney "Bargain Corner" Rosenzweig; Lt. Johnny Kelly, S.P.D.; Lem "Lumberman" Highsmith; and Johnny Ganem, restaurant owner; all recognized the visitor.

"O. K., my name is Joe DiMaggio..."

Interrupting, Meyer shot back, "Yea, and I'm Dick Tracy." Drawing laughter, creating an opening for "Bo" to

74

enter the scene. Directly confronting Meyer, whispered, "What's up?"

"Nothin', I can handle it, this guy says he's Joe DiMaggio, if he is, then I'm The Pope."

"Very good, Holy Father, you're The Pope, and he is none other than "The Yankee Clipper" Joe DiMaggio!"

"You are kiddin' me...you can't be serious?"

Now the crowd increased by 15 to 20 absolutely roared. "No, Meyer, I'm not kidding." Extending a hand to the tall, nice looking Italian youth, "Joltin' Joe DiMaggio, it is a high honor to meet you."

"Mr. Bo Peep, thank you, I brought you a photograph of the 1938 World Champion, New York Yankees, your friend "Spud" Chandler wanted you to have, he said your second and third sons are great Yankee fans, here, it's signed by "Spud," our manager, Joe Mc Carthy; Joe Gordon, Bill Dickey and "Red" Rolfe, if you will permit me, I'd like to sign it as well."

"Yes, sir, please, I'll always treasure this. I'll have it framed and put it in a place of honor...you had quite a season!"

"Yes, thank you, hit .324 with 32 home runs and 140 runs batted in...our pitching staff was stellar...Lou Gehrig and Charlie Keller were great!"

"Three World Championships in a row, wow!"

"With a little luck and God's blessings next year, we'll be right there again, and maybe make it four in a row; that would really be something big, not bragging, mind you, health of the team is a prime factor. So, we will see."

"See ya' fellows..."

"Now, let's see, where were we? Is it Pope Meyer the First, or Pope Pinzer?"

"Tiger, don't forget, make his check payable to Pope Meyer, The First, and mail it direct to the Vatican, they'll know what to do with it! You know better than anyone, that The Pope takes a vow of poverty."

"Meyer, please don't wear your crown behind the register, the players might not understand! Now, if it's alright with you, let's go back to work, the show is over for today!"

CHAPTER FOUR

As World War, II, was drawing to a close, "Bo" promised, as a celebration, he'd take some of "the boys," to the world famous Kentucky Derby. Plans were formulated early in 1945, became a frequent topic of conversation. Generally speaking, the Derby is held on the first Saturday in May, but this year the government imposed a war time ban on racing, and threatened to cancel the big race. However, following VE Day, on May 8, government announced that the ban was lifted, and, that the Seventy-first Derby could be run June 7, of that year. "Bo" invited twelve of his closest friends, gamblers all, to accompany him, all expenses paid, to the Derby in Louisville, Ky. A bus with driver was rented from a local bus company, and, on Friday morning at 6:00 A.M., "the lucky thirteen," departed on the journey. Food and beverages were provided, arrangements for a full day of activity were made, including visits to the barn area, walk around smelling hay, horseflesh and manure; watch exercise boys work snorting, steaming horses out on the track; meet and talk with trainers and jockeys. Lodging was provided at the luxurious, old, Brown Hotel in downtown Louisville, center of pre-race festivities.

"Big Buster" Gertlieb, a huge six foot, ten inch, 300 pound man with a loud, booming voice, was first on the bus, carrying a loaf of fresh baked rye bread, sack of oranges, jar of kosher dill pickles, six home made kosher corned beef sandwiches. He talked continuously, providing information about "everything Kentucky," most of which was ignored by the others. His mission, in addition to "breaking the bank at Churchill Downs," was to obtain the recipe for a "Black Screwdriver." A combination of orange juice, Jack Daniels sour mash bourbon liquor. Another was to learn the secret of a good "Mint Julep," official drink of the Derby. Two ounces of straight bourbon whiskey, fresh mint and finely crushed ice in a tall glass. The "real secret" of the Julep is to carefully strip leaves from the stem, so that it doesn't make the drink bitter. Imagine waking up Derby morning and gulping down a "Mint Julep" before breakfast, for many that is breakfast.

When asked how he felt to be going to his first Derby, "Big Buster," said, "Like going to a party!"

"Ferdie" Brennaman was so excited his speech impairment and stuttering increased to a higher level. It took him two minutes to say, "Go, go, go, go, goo, goo, gud, mo, mo, mor, mor, morning, evy body." Harry "The Yid" Hatman said, "I sure don't want to be standing in line behind that crazy bastard, when he tries to bet on a race. It'll be over before he gets it out!" "Ferdie" kept his money in a brown paper bag, so he would not attract attention when betting. His mother told him not to talk to strangers, which included every body, because he had no friends except "Bo." He clutched that bag with both hands.

Louie "Green Eyes" Lipmann was present, and he, too, was "pleased as pudding," to be included; as it was his first time in eleven years away from his wife. "It's nice to have some peace and quiet," was his only statement during the entire ride up to Louisville. Funny how he was completely oblivious to the loud talking and singing going on around him. That look of contentment said it all.

High point of the trip occurred when the host stood at front of the bus and told the story about how he acquired the nick name of "Bo Peep." "Ponzie" Mamalakis said, "I didn't know that was a nick name, I thought it was your real name. Golly Moses!" It is unfortunate they did not have video recorders in those days, that trip alone could have been the source of a new situation comedy on television. Show it like it was, no gag writers necessary, no taped audience reaction. If those characters didn't make you laugh, you did not have a sense of humor. Jackie Gleason was "a natural," for one lead. "And away we go!"

The Kentucky Derby is an American sporting institution. People from around the world gather to witness two minutes of exciting thoroughbred horse racing, and, to party in the grand Kentucky style. Country ham and biscuits, and Kentucky Burgoo are favorite snacks, Mint Juleps by far, the favorite drink, including water.

Pretty woman abound, all types; statuesque beauties, petite maidens, country girls; dressed in everything from blue jeans and cotton blouses to imported silk dresses from the fashion centers in Europe, and hats of all kinds, shapes, color and designs. A beautiful, bewildering feast for the eyes.

The Derby always has been a raucous event, so naturally it was looked forward to in anxious anticipation by the "lucky 13," none of whom had witnessed it in person.

The group met Colonel E. R. Bradley, the breeder, whose "Idle Hour Farm," enjoyed unprecedented successes in the 1920's and 1930's. "Bo" inquired of the Colonel, "Do you gamble on horse races?" "I gamble on anything," the gentleman said, "I am a speculator, race horse breeder and sportsman." "Bo" responded, "You are a man after my own heart!" They also met Grantland Rice and Damon Runyan, two of the nation's most famous sports writers. Both of whom were invited to "Bo Peep's" the next time in town. "You'll feel at home!" As post time approached for

79

"The Greatest Two Minutes in Sports," "the lucky 13," were reading *The Daily Racing Form* and "tip sheets," as aids in selecting winners.

"Bo" had met Eddie Arcaro several times, picked his mount, "Hoop, Jr." Arcaro rode in thirteen Derby's, achieving a record five winners. "Banana Nose," was truly one of the greatest jockeys of all times.

"Hoop, Jr." owned by Fred W. Hooper, who purchased the colt at Keeneland's first yearling sale in 1943 for $10, 200.00. The first thoroughbred purchased by Hooper, took an easy, smooth, early lead and stayed in front all the way, winning by six lengths, over a muddy track, in winning time of 2:07, was trained by I. H. Parke. After all the shouting and tumult died down, "Bo" led "the boys" to the pay window to collect his rather nice profit. Win ticket paid $9.40; place $5.20; show $4.00. He had bet $600.00 "across the board." "Pot O' Luck" was second, and "Darby Dieppe," came in third. (Statistical information supplied by *The Daily Racing Form.*) A good time was had by all, "the lucky 13," happy but exhausted, partied all night, on the way home.

Monday, upon returning, Meyer and "Tiger," greeted the smiling victor, and questioned, "How much did you bet for us?" "Same amount you gave me!" "Well," Meyer said, "I didn't give you nothin', cause I was in short pants." "Bo," responded, "Maybe next time you'll have long pants with deep pockets!" Johnny chewed his cigar, grimaced, and went to the bank. As a side note, the second son also picked "Hoop, Jr." giving $10.00 of his savings to "Daddy" to bet. Possibly creating an initial interest in what was to become a life long passion and love for thoroughbreds.

"It was over too soon. Just think; that was a chance of a life time, in a life time of chance!"

Each succeeding year "the boys" gathered at 19 East Congress, to reminisce and recall the numerous occurrences of that "terrific trip." Somehow, the money they won increased every year, but, whose counting?

CHAPTER FIVE

Baseball Spring Training was always fun and exciting, as some Major League teams gathered in Florida for training, exercise, and inter-league exhibition games. Yankees, Dodgers, Athletics, Giants, Phillies, Cardinals, Orioles and others set up camp early in January. That was the time of year, "kids" and "prospects" tried out for various teams, and, as a result, Savannah was a half-way stop, as travel by bus was the accepted mode.

It was during Spring of 1945 that Jerome Herman "Dizzy" Dean stopped in to visit "Bo Peep's."

"Dizzy Dean was a man of many accomplishments and even more words, some of which, actually, good English.

The National League's last thirty game winner was a member of the St. Louis Cardinals, "Gas House Gang." A big, tall, "good ol' country boy," with a great, warm personality, good sense of humor, king sized appetite. After introducing himself to every one in the establishment, he and "Bo Peep" partook of lunch in the restaurant. "Dizzy" ordered "one of them famous roast beef sandwiches, with a double order of mashed potatoes and a cup of coffee," consumed it in good fashion, proceeded into the billiard parlor to talk about "the grand ol' game."

Proud, boastful, however, he made good on his boasts. As he put it, "It ain't bragging if you can do it."

First Major League appearance was in 1930, but was sent down to the Texas League, and in 1932, returned to the Cardinals, where he paced the National League in innings pitched, strikeouts and shutouts.

In 1933 he won 20 games and again led the National League in strikeouts. On July 30, 1933 he struck out 17 Chicago Cubs setting a now broken modern major league record. In 1934 he was joined in St. Louis with his brother, Paul "Daffy" Dean, also a pitcher. In January, 1934, "Dizzy" predicted a National League Championship for St. Louis. "How are they goin' to stop us," he boasted, "Paul's going to be a sensation, he'll win 18 to 20 games. I'll count 20 to 25 for myself. I won 20 last season, and I know I'll pass that figure."

Yup, pass it he did. In 1934 the Cardinals won the pennant and "rookie" Paul Dean won 18. "Dizzy" went an astounding 30 and 7.

On September 21, 1934 the Dean brothers pitched at Ebbets Field, in a double-header against the Brooklyn Dodgers. In the first game "Dizzy" carried a no-hitter into the eighth inning and beat Brooklyn 13 – 0, on a three hit gem. In the second game, Paul pitched a no-hitter, allowing only a first inning walk. "If I'd known what Paul was gonna do, I woulda pitched one too," "Dizzy" commented. That same year, in the World Series against the Detroit Tigers, "Diz" predicted, "Me and Paul'll win two games apiece." Really? Right, again, "Dizzy" won game one and seven; Paul won game three and six. (Statistics provided by *The Sporting News.*)

In 1937, over his protestations, "Dizzy" appeared in the All-Star Game, and in the third inning, as fate decreed, Earl Averill lined the ball off Dean's left, little toe, fracturing it. "Fractured, Hell!! The damned things broken!!" Dean said in an interview on radio.

He remained in baseball as both a player and coach until June, 1941, when he began broadcasting St. Louis Cardinals and St. Louis Browns games for Falstaff Beer.

"Dizzy's" disregard for "good English" caused considerable consternation. St. Louis Board of Education demanded that he be taken off the air. "Dizzy" Dean wasn't phased and didn't move. "Let the teacher's teach English, and I'll teach baseball." As for use of "ain't" he said, "There is a lot of people in the United States who say isn't, and they ain't eatin'." Frequently used another pet word, "he slud into second base!"

Elected to The Hall of Fame in 1953, Dean informed his standing room only audience, "The good Lord was good to me. He gave me a strong body, a good right arm, and a weak mind."

He became a national figure doing games on the Mutual Network, "Game of the Day," which was broadcast on over 500 stations during the 1950's.

In 1953 he did TV games on the ABC Network as "The Game of the Week." A huge hit, pulling in 75 percent of all viewers in non-big league cities. By the end of the 1950's, Dean, according to his partner "Buddy" Blattner was "A national figure, one of the best known and most loved people in the nation; not just in sports, - in the entire nation." Dean made national polls showing him to be on the "Most Recognizable List." In 1955 the "Game of the Week," moved to CBS- TV. Blattner was Dean's partner from 1955 through 1959, then "Pee Wee" Reese succeeded him in 1960 through 1969. "Who'd thunk it?" "Ol' Diz" was the man, did the game descriptions, "Pee Wee" provided "color." Together they were as entertaining as could be, especially when "Dizzy" talked about the times and team mates. Listeners smiled as they heard Dean say "PEEE WEEE," in that southern drawl.

Well, here we are in Spring of 1945, with "The Greatest Pitcher of All Time, parading around, meetin' n greetin' folks." Bigger than life.

"Ol' Diz" was eager to meet the men, and moved directly to the cigar counter, where he quickly indulged Meyer in conversation. He instructed how to throw a curve ball and a fast ball. Meyer watched intently, seized the baseball and responded by showing "Dizzy" how to throw a "sneeze ball," placing the ball under his ample nose, sneezed on it, then spit it on it, "Pa-tooey!" As a follow-up he also illustrated how to throw "the Matzo Ball." At the conclusion of which, "Dizzy" laughed so hard, he brought tears to his eyes. "Man, you are somethin' else!" Then, without warning, "Dizzy" removed his boot to show the toe that had been "broke."

During a broadcast from St. Louis, later that year, "the boys" decided to send a telegram to "Dizzy", who was doing "play-by-play" between the St. Louis Cardinals and New York Giants. Telegram advised: "The boys at Bo Peep's are listening and enjoying your broadcast." "Diz" read the telegram over the air, and stated: "THIS BO PEEP AIN'T NO FAIRY TALE!!"

His autographed picture bearing the inscription, "Best Wishes to Bo Peep and all the boys," hung in a place of honor for several years, behind the cigar counter.

The world was a sadder place when he died in 1974. Radio and TV stations presented comment, editorials and biographical sketches.

Jerome Herman "Dizzy" Dean, - "May he Rest in Peace."

CHAPTER SIX

Halloween, 1949, few of "the boys" got together and talked about, what else, sex, feminine gender, or, girls, and, their individual sex appeal or lack thereof. They were all about 20 or 21 years old and naturally had healthy sexual appetites. Around 6:30 P.M., "Ruben" asked the group if anyone had played "Wang Dang Doo?" The fellows had not heard of that game, let alone play it. Whereupon "Ruben" says, "Well, young men, let's all go to the Alamo Motel tonight to play!"

"Charlie," who had very poor eyesight, was especially anxious, because he could not play basketball and baseball or other games the boys played. "You can count me in!"

"Abie" and the other two were a little reluctant, not knowing what in Hell they were going to do, but he knew "Ruben" well enough, that it couldn't be all bad, so he nodded his assent, and the others followed, "O. K., let's play!" 8:30 P.M. was the time agreed upon to meet at Alamo Motel, located on East Bay Street.

"Ruben" arrived early, rented a room for $19.00 and prepared for the game. Producing an amazing contraption, comprised of an old wagon wheel, sixty inches diameter; a pole or rod, mounted on a wood frame. Assembled, the wheel rotated freely on the pole.

Next, he called "Indian Lil," who, for many years operated a first class whore house, without interference from police types; on Indian Street, in "the port city." She, a handsome woman, five feet, eight inches tall, dark hair, green eyes, 38 years of age; that kept fifteen to twenty clean, white, girls busy in "world's oldest profession."

Saturday night, and paydays, one could observe some of Savannah's most distinguished, upstanding gentlemen visiting "Lil's" for a "little strange." Occasionally lines formed. More experienced "Don Juans" called ahead for appointments, similar to doctors or dentists offices; indicating particular girl, sexual preference, estimated time of arrival as well as departure. Lillian left nothing to chance, operated in professional, efficient manner. Rode herd on the "girls" making sure they maintained personal cleanliness, without disease of any type including head colds; keeping "health card" current; refrained from drinking alcohol on premises, no profanity. In other words, a nice place to visit.

One "girl" was ordered for the evening at a total cost of $100.00. At 8:00 P.M. a rather attractive young wench, about twenty-five years old, arrived and "Ruben" explained that she was going to engage in a game, "Wang Dang Doo!" "Rachel" examined the equipment, smiled broadly, agreed to participate for $100.00 cash, money up front. "I understand, but, you know, it's your thang, do whacha' wanna do." "That's great, here's your cash."

Four excited "boys" showed up promptly, "Ruben" told them they could play "Wang Dang Doo" for $25.00 each, and that it was an incredible new game, wherein they tied the girl's wrists, with her approval, to spokes on the wheel, above her head, in a comfortable position; spread her legs apart, tie her ankles to spokes on bottom of wheel, permitting her to stand on inside of rim. Thus protruding her "private part," resembling a large letter X. Certainly "Ruben's" engineer training came in handy.

Lights were dimmed, and only one small table lamp illuminated the objective. Boys will be boys, which, in this situation, they began acting silly, and pushing each other around, suggesting who should go first, and who goes last. As might be expected, "Charlie" jumped to first place in line, and said "I'll show you how!" It didn't work out that way, "Charlie" got lost, and did not find "the honey spot." "Damn it, Damn it!"

Guys waited their turns, while "playing with themselves," and watching friends approach with penis erect, penetrate "Rachel," "Rube" turned the wheel slowly – it usually took one complete revolution before ejaculation, at which time the actor had to yell, "Wang Dang DOO!!"

It was all over in twenty minutes, "Rachel" left the premises shaking her head in a disbelieving manner, muttered, "You crazy Bastards, that was a first for me." "Rube" responded, "Boys, we got a virgin!"

Next day at "Bo Peep's," that was the talk of the town, as acquaintances came in, "Rube" was quick to demonstrate the act, tell the story. Everyone screamed with laughter as he described trouble poor "Charlie" had trying to locate the "Honey Spot." "Charlie" for the first time in recent memory was lost for words, just wagged his head side to side. To this very day, any time "Wang Dang Doo" is mentioned it evokes laughter, and the oft-told story is repeated. After that faithful night, several of "Bo Peep's Boys" desired to join the "Wang Dang Doo Club." Unfortunately membership was closed. Have you heard the blues song, "Wang Dang Doo? Wonder what its about?

CHAPTER SEVEN

Memories. Memories. It seems like only yesterday in 1939, "Bo Peep" had a close personal friend named Johnny Harris, who opened a restaurant and bar on East Victory Drive in Savannah. Johnny and "Bo" were similar in more ways than one. Both were men of small statue; both came up the "hard way;" both loved their food business; both were hard working; both dedicated their lives to development of their businesses, they respected each other, both died too young.

One Sunday morning Johnny invited his pal to visit, so he could "pour his heart out." It seemed that the night before a shooting occurred between two "rowdy crackers." Sitting in the same booth, number nine, in kitchen area, where bullet holes were apparent, lamenting the woes of that night. Utterly distressed, confused as to why these "damn fools" chose his place, to "show their asses." "Thank God, nobody was seriously hurt." "Johnny, don't worry about it, everything will be fine, anybody that knows you, knows it sure had nothing to do with you or your business. Forget all about it." Harris accepted that advice, poured drinks for them to share, toasted each other. Afterwards, Johnny personally cooked fried chicken, invited criticism. Carefully explaining how chicken was selected, prepared, same weight, washed, cleaned, blanched, deep fried at 350 degrees for an exact time, in vegetable oil specially processed by SCOCO; remove, seasoned with salt and pepper from large aluminum shakers; cut into quarters, served on white bread, toasted both sides at same time in "pop-up" toaster, buttered with a paint brush.

Johnny questioned whether or not he should add other spices? "Bo" quickly answered, "Hell, No. You have the best fried chicken in the world right now, you don't need to mess with perfection." "Thanks!"

That was simply a meeting between two kings of cuisine in Savannah, one, "King of Roast Beef," the other "King of Chicken." As a small token of appreciation, Johnny presented his friend with a "brown bag of fried chicken," to carry home for Sunday dinner. They parted with a firm handshake, a warm embrace, a very sincere "Thank you, I knew I could count on you!"

Later, in 1940, while driving to his summer home on Tybee Island, "Bo" stopped on the side of the road, where a little white lady dressed in a blue, ankle length skirt, red and white checkered apron, floppy blue bonnet, perched jauntily upon her head, tied under chin. Seated behind a screen topped wood box, containing a dozen "deviled crabs," freshly prepared by her, she was trying to sell. The two exchanged greetings in polite, friendly manner; after realizing she was talking with "Mr. Bo Peep" she acknowledged, "I'm Mrs. Williams." "Please try these crabs for me, let me know what you think." Purchasing six, "the little man" said he'd return next day and give her his opinion.

After enjoying the best "deviled crab" he and his family ever tasted; next day advised the lady how enjoyable they were, and encouraged her to continue doing the same. Suggested that she "open a seafood restaurant on that same location, featuring limited menu; fried fresh local shrimp, fish, oysters, deviled crabs, cole slaw and salads. No alcoholic beverages." Offered any financial assistance he could render. She thanked him profusely, hugged his neck, bid him warm good-bye. Weeks thereafter, "Bo" was a one man advertising agency, raved to friends and associates about this ladies "deviled crabs." Her business flourished, and is continued today in the exact same location, *"Williams Sea Food Restaurant."*

"Thank you, Mr. Bo Peep."

CHAPTER EIGHT

"Hey, man, any book about Savannah, Georgia has got to have at least one chapter about women; or, at least a woman; preferably a beautiful, sexy woman; maybe even a movie star; or something like that." - Robert Mitchum, Hollywood, California. Which brings us to Tallulah Bankhead. Star of stage, screen, radio, television.
"Tell it like it is, don't hold back!"
Tallulah was born in Huntsville, Alabama in 1903. Her father, William B. Bankhead, prominent "Democrat to the Core," elected to U. S. House of Representatives, where he was honored to be named "Speaker of the House," serving in that prestigious position four years. (Life Magazine, June 25, 1951.)
Bankhead family vacationed at Tybee Island several years, during which they made friends with "Savannah's Finest," including Sol Kaminsky, Marion Faircloth, Aaron Kravitch.
A beautiful woman, Tallulah made her movie debut in a major role at tender age of eighteen. Can't help but conclude she left home while still a child. Five years later she made her stage debut in London, England; where she appeared in over ten plays. She earned "Famous Actress" status during that period. In addition, she became equally famous for her drinking, drug abuse, and numerous affairs with both men and women. In fact, Tallulah was a real "party animal and Hell raiser."
One little known detail of her amazing career is that she was "first choice among established stars," to play the coveted role of "Scarlet O'Hara," in "Gone With the Wind." It was later reported that she was ruled out because

of "a bad screen test;" which, some believed, and attributed to alcohol.

In June, 1945, while "taking a break," staying at De Soto Hotel, she having received the New York Critics Award, for her role in Alfred Hitchcock's "Lifeboat," (New York Times) Tallulah consumed two bottles of liquor a day, and craving some, late one evening sought assistance of friend, Kaminsky, receiving the desired response, "I'll get what ever you want!" It was getting close to closing time, so, when in need, call "the Doctor, Gully," who understood the problem, agreed to personally deliver liquor to her suite. All dressed up in his best sport coat, cleanly shaved and doused with "smell good," the gallant man was invited in to meet Tallulah.

"Hello, daaahling!" Her famous greeting, sliding comfortably off sugar coated tongue, in that charming, gravel throated, southern accent. You could've knocked "the Doctor" over with a feather.

"You are what the doctor ordered!"

"Yes, I am the Doctor!"

The encounter was short but sweet, marking a highlight in the life of "Gully" Silver, one he always remembered, "memories are made of this."

Tallulah, without male escort, was in need, as "the boys" would say, "hot as a three dollar pistol." This most immoral female appealed to her friend again, telling him, "Last time I visited this God forsaken place, I met a most attractive man, who reminded me of Clark Gable, ...do you know who I'm referring to?"

"Looks like Clark Gable. "Let me think," calling his wife Sophie, repeating the question; "Only person I know fitting that description is a lawyer friend of mine, named "Spencer Goodhope."

"That's him, how could I forget, too much cocaine, I guess. Daaahling, be a dear, ask him to call me, I'd love to spend time with him."

"Sure, I'll call him in the morning. Good night."

Three days later, "Spencer" called Sol to thank him; mumbled weakly, "That was the damndest seventy-two hours I've experienced; made me proud I was a man!"

"Yeah, I suppose so, that's somethin' most men dream about, you can tell your grand kids, think they'll believe you?"

"You mean, if I have grand kids, Hell, no, they won't believe a word of it...I owe you one King Solomon, man of great wisdom!"

CHAPTER NINE

"The little man," was for all purposes, blind in his right eye. In 1945 he traveled to a famous cataract clinic in Marshalltown, Iowa for corrective surgery, but to no avail. Disappointed not depressed, met triumph and disaster the same. He could not drive an automobile, depended on taxis or buses for transportation to and from home.

Although he owned a restaurant, billiard parlor, bar and hotel; his major interest and chief occupation was "book making." That is, he set betting odds on sports after consultation with Frank Ericson in New York and Charlie Leb in Jacksonville, Fla. Of course this was incredibly detail work, as odds fluctuated on games, similar to stock prices on the New York Stock Exchange, and were constantly being adjusted to reflect "action" received on a particular event. As an example, Dodgers vs. Giants, major league baseball game. If "Sandy" Koufax pitched for Dodgers, they were established as favorites to win, odds were 8 to 5. That is, if you bet on Dodgers, you had to bet $8.00 to win $5.00, or a total return of $13.00. A bet on Giants was the reverse, or greater, subject to change. A bet was a bet, and did not change once accepted. So, it was possible that he take five bets on Dodgers at 8 to 5, then, to mitigate his losses, increase odds to 9 to 5, or increase Giants to 2 to 1 to attract interest or "action." Fascinating and interesting, considering there were anywhere from one to eight baseball games a day (16 teams); and he kept it all in his mind without benefit of adding machine or "computer." The ideal situation occurred when it was a "pick 'em" game; that is both teams were considered equal; you pick the winner, he set odds at 6 to 5, way either team.

Volume assured profit. Two college professors from Armstrong Junior College interviewed him on "book making," one of which was a mathematician. He was astounded and impressed with the volume, equations, percentages involved, amazed with his ability to retain it all.

Please remember, with exception of the first three grades of elementary school, he had no formal education. Self taught to read and write. Unbelievably unique, he added a double column of thirty numerals correctly, first time. Today, people use adding machines.

When a bet was made, it was written in ink by the bettor, on a small sheet of white paper, four by six inches. (Date, team, odds amount, some means of identification.) Upon receipt, "Bo" placed paper in left pocket, cash in right pocket of his pants. Usually, right one bulged with currency, that flapped back and forth as he walked. "Ruben," suggested, "He looks like a penguin." Majority of bets were placed between 10:00 A.M. and 3:00 P.M. Night games extended those hours from 3:00 to 6:30 P.M. requiring his presence.

A closet at rear of billiard parlor, with one incandescent bulb, was his "office." One chair, wood crate desk. Bets were assembled, if there was too much "action" on one event, he called New York or Jacksonville to "lay-off a piece."

Monday to Saturday, weather permitting, he left his building, crossed Congress Street, sat on the third park bench in Johnson Square, directly in front of Christ Church. Fed pigeons bread crumbs or roasted peanuts purchased from a vendor in the Square. He relished that respite, it was a ritual, he laughed, said, "I fed these same pigeons yesterday, they know a good thing when they see it."

That park bench was also an "office." Sight to behold, this little man sitting alone, feet barely touching ground; blue ball point pen in hand, right eye closed, squinting left eye peering through thick bi-focal type eye glasses, gold frames. Dressed in cotton pants, cotton shirt, left front pocket showing ink marks of a "hundred" entries. Bets were accepted over telephone from persons whose voice and name were immediately recognizable. Bet was written down by hand, that only he could decipher, sometimes so illegible, he couldn't read it. Relying on bettor to be honest and trust worthy, make bet "good" if he lost. Fiercely proud of his name and reputation, any time he sensed a "player" or "bettor" was getting in too deep, invited him out to that bench, where they discussed the situation, and, if real, cautioned against "getting in over your head." "If I feel you are in too heavy, I will refuse your action. You must be responsible and sensible, tomorrow is another day."

He loved that spot. It provided fresh air, relief from constant calls. Enabled him to see people from all walks of life, as they stopped to visit, or just wave as they passed. Peddlers, beggars, bankers. including Mills B. Lane of C & S National Bank; Clergy, Msgr. T. James McNamara, Catholic Diocese of Savannah; Rabbi George Solomon, Temple Mickve Israel; business types, Morris Levy, Morris Levy's Men Shop; Jack Levy, Levy Jewelers; Harry Riner, The Style Shop; lawyers, Shelby Myrick, Sr. and Jr.; John J. Bouhan, John Wiley, Emanuel Lewis, Aaron Kravitch, Julius Fine, William Searcey, David S. Bracker. Individuals anxious to talk about various subjects, permitted moments of relaxation, pleasure, enlightenment, to a man possessed of keen, sharp mind. Beggars, of course, received "handouts."

97

Religious and respectful of all religions, observed Jewish "High Holy Days," Christmas, by closing business. Celebrated Easter, Thanksgiving, Memorial Day, St. Patrick's Day, Labor Day.

Politics was a passion, a loyal Democrat. F. D. R. and H. S. T. his "national heroes." Always a source of financial and spiritual support for gubernatorial candidates; Mayors, District Attorneys, Sheriffs, Judges, Congressional office seekers.

Morals a favorite subject. "You can always find the biggest sinners on the front pew in the church." "Three things that can't be legislated is wine, women and song!" "Don't tell me how religious you are, show me by your deeds." Rules by which to live.

It was this and then some that drove "little man" from rags to riches. He carefully, and painstakingly adopted a course of conduct starting with renting his business location, to acquiring piece by piece, until he owned the entire property on which this business stood these many years; comprising one-half of a city block, in the heart of downtown Savannah. In 1945, just sixteen years after the "debacle in New Orleans," he was a certified "millionare." One of the very few in Chatham County, Ga.

List of likes:

Song: "Begin the Beguine."
Color: Green
Car: Cadillac
Sport: Football
Athlete: Joe DiMaggio
Place: Home
Drink: *Coca Cola*
Liquor:*Four Roses*
Food: Roast Beef, Ice Cream a close second.

This rare individual, without hesitation, could pick a "phoney" or "four flusher," out of a crowd, and was proud of it. Did not like them at all, "avoid 'em like the plague." Definitely took firm positions about it, shake his head disapprovingly, sigh. Made a point to discuss flaws like phoniness with his children, summarized feelings, "If they ain't real or genuine, play the ignore!" Several occasions he lectured "Ruben," Carl, "Bootsie," "Boogie," Seymour on experiences in that area; warning them, "don't waste your time!"

Another matter which he had an utter and complete disregard was homosexuals, "queers," "faggots." They were not welcome in his businesses, barred upon first complaint of any inappropriate conduct; asked to leave immediately, slightest delay invited physical removal. "These predators are not genuine men!"

CHAPTER TEN

Any book about Savannah, Georgia and "Bo Peep" covering 1930 to 1955 should appropriately pay tribute to leaders and friends of that era. Savannah has been a city of monuments dedicated to those who made contributions to development, establishment, improvement. Persons worthy of similar treatment follow as a "Top People's Category."

John A. Peters, Sr., a handsome Greek-American, with engaging smile, warm, affable personality, "twinkle in the eyes." Owned and operated the largest, most prestigious liquor, beer and wine wholesalers and distributors, named appropriately *"Savannah Distributing Co."* Located off West Broad Street, near the Central of Georgia Railway tracks. "Mr. Johnny," began working at an early age, honest, reliable, fair in all dealings, accumulated considerable wealth. Contributor to many, worthy, charitable institutions; any fund-raising activity usually began with him, whether religious, political or civic. Although politicians running for state and local office "ranted and raved," against "that devil rum," nevertheless, they went to see him for contributions and assistance getting out the vote. He drove Cadillac cars, though not long, as he traded almost yearly; enjoyed fine wine and imported Cuban cigars, one of which usually placed in right corner of his mouth. Well dressed, gracious, gentleman. Every inch a man, his word was his bond; loved betting on college football games, especially Notre Dame, Georgia. Saturday noon, football season, found him enjoying a roast beef sandwich before placing "a friendly little wager." "A Great Leader, to whom much is owed."

Shelby Myrick, Sr., was probably "Bo's" initial contact in the business community, as he began his career as "an errand boy" for "the elder statesman, and Abraham Lincoln of Savannah." Outstanding lawyer, able politician, community leader. This tall, lean, "country gentleman," with bright eyes, quick wit, persuasive ability, spoke with nasal twang, southern drawl. The two, genuinely liked each other, and, for over twenty-five years maintained close, personal contact, talking several times a week. "Mr. Myrick," was consulted on any important matter, and placed on monthly retainer. Numerous clients were referred to him, giving rise to a boast, "I made his law practice!" Myrick was appreciative, demonstrating that by presenting "Wolfe Silver," a large, sterling silver bowl, inscribed "to a true friend." His influence guided "Bo" through the maze of State politics, beginning with Eugene Talmadge. Myrick was one person whose judgment was unquestioned.

John J. Bouhan, lawyer, able politician, community and religious leader. "Bo's main man," in Chatham County politics. "Mr. Bouhan," was the "fellow with contacts and influence," had a reputation for "taking care of business." Political acumen and style kept him in position of power many years, resulting in benefits to both. Bouhan was "County Attorney," and "number one name on the door," at the law firm of "Bouhan, Lawrence, Williams and Levy;" offices located in heart of downtown, in Liberty Bank Building, at Bull Street and Broughton Street. Without question, these two men deserve recognition, appreciation and gratitude as "Great Leaders!"

Then, of course, Johnny Harris, founder of that landmark restaurant bearing his name, located on East Victory Drive. A quiet man that worked hard every day of his life, had a great reputation for fair and honorable dealing. He brought in his successor, Kermit "Red" Donaldson, when just a kid, "Red worked at the master's knee," learning the food and beverage business very well. When Johnny Harris answered the good Lord's call, "Red" inherited management of the enterprise and part ownership, happily the business did not miss a beat, and transference was perfect.

"Red" Donaldson was another of this select group to whom a monument should be erected in grateful appreciation of all he did to continue and perpetuate *"Johnny Harris Restaurant"* tradition of fine food, good service and pleasant atmosphere. A tall southern, honest gentleman, earnest, dedicated, with a warm, friendly personality devoted full time and attention to that business. Most days he was found in his "office," booth #1, on the left as you enter dining room and dance floor. Any complaint was immediately handled personally, to complete satisfaction of complainant. He did not permit reduction in quality, quantity or service, insisted that, "Mr. Harris did it this way, and that's good enough for me." A favorite location for prominent people, including movie and sports stars, local gentry including Chief Sidney B. Barnes, Savannah P. D; William C. "Bill" Harris, Sheriff of Chatham County; James A. Goethe, liquor distributor; J. C. Lewis, Motor Cars; George Backus, Motor Cars; J. Walter Cowart, Judge. What a pleasure visiting there, assured that it was perfect in every way. Too much good cannot be said about these two, worthy Leaders.

For many years Victory Drive has been the corridor of commercialism in the "Port City." Named In Honor of Men who served this country, who made the ultimate sacrifice, it is lined with Azaleas and Palm trees from Bull

Street east to Thunderbolt City Limits; created after World War, I. First segment was devoted to beautiful homes from Bull to Waters Avenue, many of which are still standing illustrating dedication and devotion to fine living as well as exemplary architecture. Driving in an easterly direction towards Tybee Island, as early as 1929, businesses sprung up and thrived. Passing Daffin Park on the right, Grayson Stadium, *"Rhines Florist,"* owned by Clyde Rhines over forty years; *"Joe Gildea's Bar and Grill"* owned by who else? Joe Gildea, an inimitable, delightful, entertaining fellow, that served more beer on St. Patrick's Day than anyone; did it over forty years. *"Johnny Harris Restaurant and Bar,"* supra; followed by *Al Remler's Club Royale,"* at intersection of Drive and Skidaway Road. Al Remler, Sr., was a fine gentleman of the first order, recognized at an early date, Victory Drive was special, an asset, source of progress and profit. The business bearing his name was a beautiful, modern, bar and night club, featured a large dance floor, was mecca for most famous orchestras, dance bands and entertainers, such as Guy Lombardo, Harry James, Tommy Dorsey, "Blue" Barron, Jo Stafford, Wayne King.

Taking a left turn at that intersection, immediately across the Drive was *Herb Traub's Our House Restaurant.* Traub, an astute businessman developed that location, as well as "The Pirate's House," in downtown Savannah, at foot of East Broad Street. A likable gentleman, who looked more like a college professor type, than restaurant owner, had the "golden touch," whereby his locations featured the finest food, service and quality. Jim Casey was a partner and co-developer.

Continuing in westerly direction, *The XXX Drive In Restaurant,* was a marvelous attraction on Victory Drive

103

for several years, featured indescribably delicious hamburgers, grilled cheese sandwiches, and *Hiers' Root Beer* served in twelve ounce frosted mugs by speedy, short skirted, pretty, waitresses with aluminum trays that fit in automobile window openings securely. Main gathering point for the high school crowd attending Benedictine Military School, and, "The Pape School," socially prominent, private, high school for girls. Whole bunch of hand holding, flirtations, "smacky mouth," went on there from 1939 through 1950.

It follows, that these worthy men should definitely occupy places of honor in the town's history. Clyde Rhines, Joe Gildea, Johnny Harris, Al Remler, Sr., Herb Traub, Jim Casey; each had another interesting distinction, they all were close, personal friends of "Bo Peep." Numerous occasions they relied upon his expertise, knowledge. Perhaps these names should appear on a Historical Marker along side others mentioned herein, for contributions to success and development of this very special Drive, as they dedicated and devoted their lives, fortunes to its progress, and the improvement, prosperity that was so vital to the life and future of Savannah.

Coin machine operators made large investments, not only in time, money, but also physical effort or exertion. It was a highly competitive business that required constant attention by the operators. "Bo Peep's," as an example, had one "Juke Box", six cigarette vending machines, two coin operated "pin ball" machines, two candy dispensing machines. During the 1940's through 1955, those machines yielded an average of Two Thousand Dollars per week, therefore a highly desirable venue. Jimmy "The Fat Man" Dukes, a pioneer in the field, was quick to cultivate friendship that endured over fifteen years. "Bo, I'm tellin' you that roast beef keeps gettin' better all the time! You really got somethin' special." Kind, decent, honest man that had a deep bass voice, laughed all the way down to his chest, producing a wheezing sound. They got along famously, as Jimmy came in almost daily to "rob" the machines, count coins, divide percentages. He also loaded cigarette machines, change and update 45 r. p. m. records on *Wurlitzer* or *Seaburg* brand "Juke Boxes." (One play for twenty-five cents.) Featuring stars, Frank Sinatra, Perry Como, Rosemary Clooney, Jo Stafford, "Bing" Crosby, Nat "King" Cole, Louis "Satchmo" Armstrong. Dukes, a rather rotund, "country boy," possessed a great personality, always armed with a new joke, which he enjoyed telling as much as the listener receiving it. "Did ya' hear the one about ...?" "I got another, even funnier than that one!" Contributor to many charitable causes, churches, synagogues, political campaigns. Real, legitimate character, was loved by many. As time past, his health became impaired, necessitating reduction in work schedule. After all, working eight to fourteen hours a day, in thirty different locations, numerous individuals, was sufficient to wear an "iron man" down. His most able successor was Charlie Stein, a New Yorker from "the East side," with excellent connections and credentials. Absolutely brilliant individual; outstanding businessman. About five feet, eight inches tall, 145 pounds, energetic, ambitious, human dynamo. A quiet man, but when he spoke, it was well worth listening, that accent was immediately obvious. A swell dresser, "dapper," in latest fashions, completely unlike Dukes, who preferred cotton shirts and pants. Charlie, as described by Pinzer, "Sharp as a tack." He was the first person in town to pick up on a "new stock, a company called *Polaroid*, selling for eight dollars, a share;

do yourself a favor, buy a hundred, put it away and forget about it!" "Bo" and three of his "boys" purchased a few, after a week went by, they questioned Charlie, "What's going on with that stock?" "Last time I checked, it was twenty-four, hit a high of twenty-eight! My word is my bond, if I give you my word, you can take it to the bank!" In short time, it hit forty, and split two for one, and the "boys" sold. Polaroid continued it's smashing success for several years. Charlie finally revealed after several years, the original "tip" came "direct from the horse's mouth," a friend whose name was "Land, developer of process." "Not half bad, sports fans ain't too shabby!"

That was his style, everybody that knew him respected him. He built a solid reputation, married a beautiful lady, purchased Sol Kaminsky's house in Sylvan Terrace, off White Bluff Road; drove *Cadillac* automobiles. It's interesting, that almost all of these fellows were small in statue, but big in heart. "What a guy!"

May he Rest in Peace.

Another in the top hierarchy of distinguished citizens was Hon. Peter Roe Nugent, Mayor, baker, Irish-Catholic, devoted leader, of which there were a few; likable, all-around good guy. Honestly loved the town, did his best to make it a better place to live. A born politician with big smile, hearty laugh, warm hand shake and pat on the back for everybody. Founder of one fine bakery, Nugent's Bakery, worked there for many years while making substantial contributions to the town. Perennial problem for citizens, every time it rained hard, streets flooded in many areas; he led the effort to install better sewerage systems. He'd put on a "hard hat," appear at construction sites, solve problems then and there, encourage engineers to go that one extra mile. A prince among men.

These, are a few of the really good, fine, decent men that devoted their time, effort and money to the "Imperial State of Chatham." All friends of "Bo." Each worthy of having a monument erected to their memories. When the poor cried, these men wept. They were loved by friends and families, not without just cause.

In those days, it was interesting to note how "minorities" got together at "Bo's." Great, life-long friendships were forged there. Greeks and Jews especially so. Greek population, as small as it was, made huge contributions to quality of life in our little town. Primarily small business, restaurant, clothing store owners, quality, pleasant people. Frequent visitors, Steve Andris, before he left town to operate a major dog racing facility near Tallahassee, Florida; Gus Alfieris, Paul Anestos, alderman; John Nichols, Sr. and Jr., Harry Anestos, attorney, departed for Washington, D. C., John Rousakis, Mayor; Johnny Skeadas, George Chengis. They would meet, greet and eat there; talking occasionally in their native tongue. They, like Jews, who used "Yiddish," figured it out, that sometimes you can converse when you did not want to be overheard or understood by others. Saturday afternoons sounded like a meeting of the United Nations. It's funny that curse words in foreign languages sound so nice, a lot of times you called a guy a "mumzer" and he liked it.

There was a bar in the rear of the "pool room," where five foot, two inches, Isidore "Gully" Silver presided as bar tender, singer of songs when intoxicated, "Father Confessor," master of "galloping dominoes," or dice, as some folk know them. He could throw any number on any dice, under careful scrutiny; make it look easy, and accidental like. Few "wise guys" offered him big dollars to teach them the "fine art of shooting dice," but he respectfully declined and always said, "I learned this at the University of Hard Knocks!" Come winter time "the Gull" flew south to spend a little time relaxing at Miami Beach, separating "smart fellows" from "piles of green."

A likeable little person was he, nevertheless, on one occasion, became target of a six foot, six inches, 265 pound, abusive drunk; that did everything possible to upset "the Doctor," as he was affectionately known. Finally, challenging him to, "come out in the alley, where I will kick your ass 'till you're blue in the face.!" "That did it!" "Doctor," couldn't take it any more, reached under the bar, pulled out a pool cue cut down to forty inches, containing led rod, told the guy, "After you, sir." Hit the bastard hard with right fist in belly; he buckled, then crack him across back of his head with cue. Called police, who summoned ambulance to carry guy to hospital for eight stitches. Ten days later he returned to apologize, ask forgiveness, permission to enter in "good standing." Permission denied. Whereupon the big guy cried real tears, and silently left the building, never to show his face again. "Gully" told Billy Harty, "I just don't like unruly drunks, they give the joint a bad name."

Family was important to "Bo," so it was a "no brainer," to hire "The Doctor" to operate the bar, as he was experienced, having owned a facility in Miami Beach with a "mile long bar," named *The Hippodrome.* "Izzy," was "Bo's" younger brother, they looked enough alike that anyone could detect they were brothers, same size, weight, smile. A "professional bar tender," was master of his trade, mixer of over one hundred fifty different alcoholic beverages without benefit of recipe, amazingly, results were identical every time. His hours were 2:00 P.M. 'till closing, that did not prevent him from coming early, leaving late. Blessed with good memory, knew regular customers names and drinks, upon entry, said, "What'll it be, the usual Mr. Donahue? *"Cutty"* straight, soda on the side."

Good listener, round face, receding hair line, glasses, weighed about one hundred thirty five pounds, "soakin' wet." Loved people, jokester, brilliant conversationalist, sharp, rapid fire delivery; meticulously clean, maintained the beautiful forty-five foot mahogany wood bar in immaculate, well polished, gleaming condition. Lived in *The Drayton Arms Apartments,"* downtown. Loved family, and made it a point to attend all gatherings during "high holy days."

On more than one occasion, sat at the bar's end, drink of *"Early Times"* in a "shot glass," ginger ale on the side, discussing life, what it was, and what it might have been. Sixth grade education, enjoyed talking with close, personal friends for hours. One participant, was "Big Neil" Greer, giant of a man, that exaggerated "Gully's" small statue. Neil was "Old Fort Irish," Benedictine graduate, star of Cadets football team, sought a little drink or two after work and before going home. He lived alone and apparently liked it.

"Gully," began slowly, "You know," speaking with a New York twang in his voice, two others drawing near to engage in this discussion; "Gull, before we get started, or too far into this important matter, can we have a couple of beers? *Schlitz* is O.K." The warm weather, no doubt contributed to this sudden thirst. "Comin' up, two ice cold beers, in frosted mugs, for my two pals!" "Nothin' worse than a thirsty listener." Warming to the task, "Gully" continued, "Sometimes I think I'd like to be the new Messiah."

"Now, that's a helluvah idea! I'd certainly enjoy havin' the Messiah as my friend, my associate, drinking companion. Man, I'd do what I want to, have nothin' to worry about, no problem, see my friend the Messiah, he'll fix it!"

"What a great way to get rich quick; four *Cadillacs,* six bed room house on Victory Drive, two car garage, swimming pool, movie stars as buddies; several disciples doing my biddin'. I'd dress in a long white, silk gown and robe, with a much bejeweled crown. Only thing is, I get talked into stuff too easily, that's no good, besides, who ever heard of a short, bald, middle aged Messiah with bad eyesight?" "I dunno, listening to all them people with problems is a lot like being a bar tender, and, that's what I do now!"

"Gull, you kill me! I'd like to be a full back at Notre Dame, or heavy weight fighter, somethin' self respectin', savin' sinners is too hard," Neil quickly rejoined. Messiah, though, is a whole 'nother deal."

"Have another, boys?"

"No, I think not, can't get tight tonight, my girl is getting' lucky." Neil picked up a hard-boiled egg out of a white ceramic bowl, cracking it by rolling it along the solid mahogany topped bar, and walked out into the sultry evening; "You know, Gull, shave and wash your face, you might really do good as the new Messiah!"

Other listeners looked a little surprised, however, they did not laugh.

"What a guy, magnificent wasn't he?" Tony Flanigan said quietly as Neil departed.

"Seems like Neil found a new friend, orders anyone?"

"Gull, what time do the dancin' girls come in?"

"Not tonight, only second Tuesdays of each week, but we can watch T.V...."

"That's about all we can do, you got the sound turned down so damn low,...."

"Don't wanna interfere with customer's thinkin', and, you know, you seen one Phil Silvers' you seen 'em all!"

"No kidding?"

"No kidding!"

"Frankly speaking, I'd rather go outside and watch parking meters expire, it's a lot more fun and educational too!"

"Be my guest, that heat is unbearable...see ya' fellows, don't take no wooden nickels!"

"Nah, not if I can help it."

"Me, neither,...Gull, take care...see you tomorrow, if the good Lord's willing...and I'm able!"

CHAPTER ELEVEN

During World War, II, from 1941 – 1945, "Bo Peep's" became a mecca for servicemen in the Army, Navy, Coast Guard, Marines and Air Force. The host was quick to welcome, make them comfortable, opening his heart, mind, home and business. Groups of up to forty were entertained at his Tybee Island residence. Many a lonesome fellow poured his heart out, some crying, which caused tears in return. In appreciation, several plaques, citations, commendations, tributes were awarded and graciously received. A heavy bomber was named "Bo Peep's Blastin' Bastards!" As Sol Kaminsky, owner of the Cadillac-Pontiac Agency in Savannah, eloquently put it, - "No man ever gave so much, to so many, asked so little in return." On numerous occasions small loans were made, without interest, to tide them over to pay day. Letters, gifts from all over the world acknowledged his kindness. Envelopes simply addressed, BO PEEP – Savannah, Ga. Photos of groups and individuals in uniform, with and without ladies; in tanks, "Jeeps," aircraft, ships. He was "best man" in several weddings, witness to wills and real estate deeds.

A true visionary, a man before his time, best described him.

In 1941, when the world was plunged into war; Georgia, due to Senator Richard B. Russell's influence, became a military training center. Camp Stewart, in Hinesville, Ga., forty miles west of Savannah, was being constructed hastily in the insect, snake infested "bog hole." Traveling there early in construction phase, "Bo" learned the exact location of the Main Gate. He, alone, purchased property on both sides of the dirt road, and began constructing a rectangular wood framed building to be used for a bar, restaurant and dance floor on one side, and a barbecue restaurant on the other. Hired local folks to operate the businesses, and got acquainted with the "High Sheriff of Liberty County, Paul Sikes." Paul was the adventurous type, took an immediate liking to "the little man from Savannah." In fact, they were so close, Paul permitted exclusive installation of fifty slot machines in each location. Nickel, dime and quarter machines purchased from manufacturers in New York and Chicago, all being mob-related, run predominantly by Al Capone in Chicago, and Vincent Mangano in New York.

My goodness, what a little gold mine that was!

Think about counting 20,000 nickels by hand, with just the aid of a small wheel type device that spun coins in counter-clockwise motion into a metal tube containing a brown paper coin wrapper, forty nickels per wrapper. Second son soon learned value of a nickel. Some days during summer vacation from school, he counted them for hours, while everyone else was at the beach. What a great time on a hot day.

Col. William B. Ochs started out as Commanding Officer of Camp Stewart. He was elevated to Commanding General, a valued, cherished friend of "Bo." Ochs, was son of the founder of *The New York Times*, Adolph "All the news that is fit to print" Ochs. Graduate of The Military Academy at West Point, heir to a massive fortune, a frequent visitor and guest not only at his home, but also the business. These friendships were carefully developed and cultivated. Good times were had by all!

Boss of "the Gambino family in New York," Vincent Mangano represented real stability for "the family," as he was "the Man," in control from 1931 to 1951. Visited

Savannah several times, to show appreciation for "the business." Slot machines were having difficult times in "the big Apple," as law enforcement used them as good public relations, whereby they kicked down doors of private clubs, with news paper camera men standing by, taking photographs that appeared on front pages, under headlines, "Major Bust Puts Crimp in Crime!" So, naturally, if they were used elsewhere, it was a big help to Mangano. A diminutive man, typical tough Italian, came up through the ranks, the hard way; talked with a deep throated, raspy voice, gave the distinct impression that HE was Boss, "and don't you forgetit!" "Hey, Bo, don't you wanna move to Las Vegas, I got a nice little place in heart of downtown named, appropriately enough, *The Silver Slipper*. You can get in for next to nothin', we'll provide license, and of course, protection. Skys the limit." (1950.) Send someone out to have a look-see. Nothin' ventured, nothin' gained. If you need some front money its available, it'll take around Fifty "G's" to pop the cork. Send that kid of yours, that I met, we'll have someone meet him at the plane, take care of him, show him around, introduce him to good people."

"Vincent, I'll think it over, that's a helluvah idea, let me sleep on it, and I'll get back to you in a day or two."

"Bo" hurried home to discuss the matter with his second son, just turned 21 years old, and eager to be of any service to his father, "You don't have to ask me, if it's O.K. with you, it's O. K. with me, my God, just to see the western part of U.S. is a marvelous opportunity!"

Around this same period of time, "city fathers" of Savannah were approached to permit installation of slot machines in private clubs in town, such as "The Oglethorpe Club," "The Eagles Club," "The Owls club." "Bo" advised

114

them in detail of the great benefit, not only to Clubs, but also tourist trade, predicting that, "Las Vegas, Nevada, would be the biggest city in America." Machines were approved and installed in several locations for a brief period of time, then, without warning, politicians got too greedy, wanted it all. Nice guys, these politicians. They wanted all profits, without investing one cent. "Sorry, fellows, I can't go along with that!" Shortly thereafter, machines were removed, shipped to a "better" environment. Some politicians returned to say, "We really didn't mean we wanted it all!"

Too bad, Savannah. Atlanta was smart; they permitted them.

The fact of the matter was, slot machines were up and running at numerous locations throughout Savannah Beach (Tybee Island) including "The Tybee Hotel," "Tybresia Pavilion," "T. J. McCarroll's Novelty Bar," "Willie Haar's Brass Rail Lounge," "Solms Hotel," and "T.S. Chu, Variety Store, where kids aged 10 to 12 years of age were permitted to play. Consequently, it was not a stretch to imagine, that, with a little effort, Tybee could, very well become what Atlantic City, New Jersey, is now, a year-round tourist attraction. That was the vision the "little man" had. After all, liquor, beer and wine was sold openly by the drink or bottle, seven days a week, including Sundays, after church, of course. Church-goers couldn't wait for services to get over, please, so they could hurry to their favorite bar to quench thirst, soothe tongues tired from praying. Lord, Help Us!

What else can be said for Tybee? "The Brass Rail" featured top entertainers during summer, including Harry

James, "His Trumpet and Orchestra;" Jo Stafford, Rosemary Clooney, Bob and Ray Eberly, "The Sentimental Gentleman of Swing," Tommy Dorsey; "Blue" Barron; Dean Hudson, countless others. It unquestionably, undoubtedly was the place to be seen, when school was out and kids on vacation, escaping that awful, swelter zone, Savannah. "Bo" met with Willie Haar on three occasions to discuss attracting *Sheraton Hotel Corp.* and other major hotel companies to Tybee for purpose of constructing a one hundred fifty room resort hotel, complete with golf course, tennis courts, Olympic size swimming pool, on land near The Brass Rail. Several *Sheraton* officials spent five days there, preparing preliminary drawings, estimates, artist renderings, only to be discouraged by apparent lack of interest exhibited by Beach "leadership." "These folks are impossible to talk with, showing total disregard for quality development of this Island. What a shame," one spokesman from a national hotel chain proclaimed at a private meeting.

"The Imperial State of Chatham," Savannah Beach, Tybee Island, missed a golden opportunity, could have had it all, instead, the beautiful little Island "went to Hell in a hand basket," certainly struggling financially for many years; due in major part to a tiny tax base derived from part-time residents, and a few small, locally owned businesses. It brings to mind, "the gang that couldn't shoot straight;" or, "the cowboy who shot himself in the foot."

CHAPTER TWELVE

Saturdays were big at "Bo's." Students home from college. Businessmen came in to relax, listen to whatever sporting event being broadcast, watch the ticker for scores, shoot pool or billiards, eat, drink, or just observe the table action.

It seems like only yesterday, listening to that plaintive Alabama twang of Mel Allen singing the praises of the New York Yankees. Listen: "Yogi Berra steps into the batters box, digs in, adjusts his cap, stares at the pitcher Early Wynn, the wind up, the pitch, Yogi swings, there it goes into deep left field, way back, it's going, going, gone...a two run homer! How about that?" So distinct, so colorful, so entertaining.

In May, 1953, "Ruben" took an interest in the "second son," teaching him the finer points of pool. "English," "Draw," "Cut," "Bank," "Break." Up until that time the young man could shoot, but certainly not well enough to play for money. After several weeks of instruction, pupil was pronounced "ready to play for green."

Along came a fellow that "Rube" did not especially like, looking for some "action," inviting several guys to shoot a game or two. No one accepted, so "Rube" offered to play him, the man said, "No, you could beat me with one hand tied behind your back." "Well, then play this young man a game of Nine Ball, even." If you can't beat him, you should hang up your cue stick." Harold Sailor, traveled for a living, selling men's clothes. He challenged the young man to a game of Nine Ball, for $10.00. The "kid" lost the game. Harold was happy, laughing and telling jokes. Winners tell jokes, losers say, "Rack Boy, set 'em up

117

again." The "kid," excitedly, warming to the task, won the second game, when Harold missed an easy shot on the Nine Ball. "Little Boy BLEW," "Rube" stated, smiling all the while. "Kid" was too polite to laugh or tell jokes as Harold was ten years his senior. Harold says, "Let's play two more games for Twenty Dollars each." "Kid" could not afford that much, so "Rube" chimed in, "I'll bet on the "kid" on the side, Ten Dollars." Offer was accepted confidently; "O.K., Rack Boy!" Henry Noble Farmer, a black man, was the "Rack Boy" for for years, was approaching 55 years of age. He maintained the 18 tables, clean and level, kept the 165 cue sticks in top condition.

As the third game began, Julius "The Champ" Kaminsky, owner of Southern Motors, Nash Agency; Louis "The Senator" Black, a Real Estate Broker; and two others gathered to watch. Julius, clutching a bag of sunflower seeds, eating and spitting shells on the floor. Luckily "Kid" won the game. "Lucky, lucky, lucky," was all Harold said. "Rube" winked at his pupil, saying, "Yes, he sure is lucky." Fourth game, same results. At that point, Harold, called "Rube," "Cheap, no guts!" "If you think this "Kid" can beat me, you're out of your mind. Let's play for Forty Dollars a game!" "Rube," winked at the "Kid" again, frowned, said, "Why don't you quit? I don't think you can beat him. I wish I had his luck."

That did it. Harold got hot as Hell, shouting, "I ain't quitting, I can beat him blind folded." "Then, you're on, I'll take the bet," Rube responded emphatically.

Fifth and sixth game went to the "Kid." Who, now was a crowd favorite, and loving every minute of it. Louis Black whispered, "Just be cool, don't get up tight, I wish I could get a piece of the action."

Then, things got real tense. Harold shouting, "I'll play for a hundred dollars a game, now we'll see how good he is!" "Kid," realizing pressure was mounting, said, "No, I can't play for that much, but, maybe for fifty and let "Rube" in for fifty." "O. K." Several other patrons stopped playing to watch what was becoming a spectacle.

Harold lost three straight, after the final one, moaned, "I'm broke, I gotta go cash a check." "O. K., we'll wait." About 7:30 poor Harold returned with more cash, however, "Kid" and company had left the building.

That night, "Rube," feeling very generous and a little proud of his student, treated him and two of the "boys," to dinner at *"Johnny Harris' Restaurant."* "Boys, we got a new horse in the barn, maybe a front runner, but at least he finished in the lead." "Rube, you know, I couldn't have done it without you, you handled that matter like a master, and, I'm real proud to be under your wing." A great time was had by all; after dinner, "Rube" said, "Kid, come back next week, and we'll get Harold again!" "Yes!"

Frequently, "wise guys" from New York came through town, working their way south to Miami, looking for some "chump" to play. Dressed in pegged leg pants, leather jacket, wool cap, carrying their own, personal, hand made pool cue in a black carrying case. You could see 'em coming a mile away, talking that "Yankee" talk, walking that "Yankee" walk. Kinda like a baboon. Smart fellows, who knew everything, believed New York was the world, and every where else, "the sticks." "Hicks lived in sticks." The type fellow that was cruising for an ass-kicking. Upon entry, "Bo" called "Statesboro," "The Stick," or "Rube" to determine if he "Got game."

On one occasion "The Stick," played a guy for an hour, won all his money, jacket and watch. Every time the

119

"visitor" missed a shot, one of the "Boys" said, in a derisive manner, "Too bad!" Last time anyone saw "Broadway," he was standing alone at the city limits, thumbing a ride south on U. S. Highway 17. Prince turned pauper!

Feeling of friendship, fellowship and affection was evident in closeness of the "boys." Approximately sixty of them, each unique in his own way, with character and integrity. A person you proudly called "friend." Any time a "beef" arose, or an outsider overly aggressive, one or more stepped forward to handle the situation, and, if necessary go into the alley behind the building to settle it. Without exception, the "boy" won, usually in short order. "Big John" Heintz, six foot three inches all man, hit one "big mouth" on the chin so hard, he lifted him eight inches off the ground and knocked him out of his shoes! In a high pitched, girl like voice admonished, "Don't come back!"

Colorful characters abounded. Moses "Cowboy Baby" Eichholz, visited the bar weekly, to sip a drink of whiskey, or two, on a stool at the mahogany topped bar, sing "Minnie the Moocher," "Ace in the Hole," or "As Time Goes By." Couldn't carry a tune in a bucket, but that didn't matter. Talked about every body he knew, except his Mother, "Mrs. Eichholz." Left the University of Georgia Law School where he was one of six founders of Tau Epsilon Phi fraternity, to join the Navy in the early 40's. Discharged honorably with a disability pension for "nerves." When he felt he was going to drink too much, gave his check to "Bo" or the "Doctor," for safe keeping, with instructions not to let him spend it all. An admirer of "ladies with nice boobies," he sat like a cat in a fish house, offering drinks or dinner. When he got lucky, gentle man that he was, take her home in a taxi, or drive his black, Ford pickup truck, condition permitting. Some nice ladies lived with him for weeks or months. "Cowboy Baby," was an imposing figure, six feet tall, 265 pounds, bald head polished to perfection, with waste-line protruding above belt line that highlighted his cowboy pants, shirt and hat. Talked with that distinctive "Geechee" accent, except when intoxicated, then "baby talk." His constant reminder, smiling, "I'm Mrs. Eichholz's son, and have plenty of money. She owns half of Savannah including West Broad Street." Had an absolute fetish about woman who smoked, or had ugly teeth. "They smell bad, or, they can't smile pretty." Confronted by that type, doffed his ever present baseball cap or cowboy hat, wipe his sweaty bald head with palm of his hand, saying, "I think I hear someone calling me!" Or, ask "Gully," "Is Mister Bo looking for me? I taught I heard him, but I'm not sure." (Wink, wink.) "It sure is hot in here, I'll go for a walk, be back later, if I get any calls, tell them I'm gone." Anything that came to mind, to escape without offending. Proceeded to "Gully," whisper, "She got ugly teeth, please cover me, I will leave, come back later, in an hour, keep my money." Exiting, pulled his hat down far as it went, look up and down the alley, as if he were secret agent man, walk hurriedly to his truck, parked illegally in the alley, look both ways again, wave at any body he might see, even the unknown, smile and say, "See ya'." Which conduct always elicited comment from any bystander, "That is the damnedest thing I have ever seen. He must be crazy." "Doctor" responds, "Yeah, crazy like a fox."

God help any pedestrian in his way, two honks, if you ain't gone, you history. Glove compartment filled with unanswered traffic citations, on a full moon appeared at ticket office in City Courthouse, tell them, "There must be some misteak. I'm disabled war veteran, Mrs. Eichholz's son...maybe someone was using my truck." So it goes. That little conversation slipped out of my mind till much later. Well, there it was; and when you come to think of it, a pretty kettle of fish, too.

In the mid forties through forever, Savannah's premier show promoter and sponsor of entertainment was none other than C. J. "Buster" White, inimitable, exuberant, five foot, five inches tall, super salesman and human dynamo. "I can sell ice to Eskimos!" "Believe it!" He promoted everything and everybody from Opera and Ballet, to *The Grand ol' Opry,*" wrestling, boxing, Broadway Shows, popular music. You name it, he done it. His contacts were legion, always recipient of first call from New York, Nashville, Los Angeles. Daily, he checked into "Bo's" to sell tickets right out of his pocket, also assign tickets for sale at the location, swapping in return, advertisement on bill boards, placards, newspapers.

Most frequently the venue was the Municipal Auditorium. There was very little he didn't promote, however, his first love was boxing. "The Art of Pugilistic Entertainment." That gave him the license to do what he wanted to do, in his own way. "Irish" Tommy Keene, "Dedi" Mathews, Joe Dinerman, all from Savannah, entered many appearances for "Bust" as he was affectionately called by "Bo." During World War, II, he obtained servicemen from nearby armed forces, provided training facilities and offers of stardom, as well as cash. One lucky such individual was a young Mexican stationed at Camp Stewart, Hinesville, Georgia; a nice looking, clean cut, young man, with broad shoulders and good muscular development destined to be a crowd pleaser. Triumphant in his first ten fights, almost all by knock outs, earned

considerable local following among the sporting gentry.
Fact was great animosity existed between various branches
of service, was not lost upon "Buster." Scheduled a Marine
from Paris Island, South Carolina, to fight a Seaman from
Jacksonville Naval Air Station, Jacksonville, Florida.
Cognizant that each brought a contingent of followers.
Competition was fierce between the two groups, fights
broke out in the audience requiring a dozen Military Police,
and, ten local police, to quell the disturbance, restore order.
"Buster" loved every minute of it. "Isn't that awful," he
was overheard saying, while biting his tongue to prevent
laughing. "I can't believe something like this can happen!"

Admission prices at the Auditorium was $1.50,
Balcony; $5.00 Dress Circle; $10.00 Ringside, consisting
of twenty folding chairs on front row, each side of the
"squared circle," five additional rows behind. Of course,
ringside was dominated by "high rollers," real sporting
figures, and the elite.

Referee, Joe McGee, also served as ring announcer
when needed. Judges were three of "Buster's" warm,
personal friends, authorized by the Savannah Boxing
Commission. But to get back to "Buster." Kept busy
running all over town, talking up the event, handling public
relations, advertising, personally selling tickets, always for
"cash," maintaining a roll of bills six inches thick in his
right hand, front, pants pocket. "These are the best seats in
the house, you can't miss this, the winner is going to get a
title shot, one of the greatest fights you've ever seen. I
guarantee it." Or, "Come on, everybody's gonna' be there,
I saved the last four ringsides for you, right next to Mr.
Johnny Peters, Sr...." "Buster," real, honest to God,
character.

Wrestling, then as now, was fabulous entertainment, featuring villains "Black Jack" Dillon, Masked Marvel, "Bone Crusher" Beamon; and on the other side, the good guys, "Tarzan" White, "Two Ton Tony" Galensky, "The Gorgeous One, Gorgeous George." "Black Jack" Dillon, from Pittsburgh, Pa., weighed in at 219 pounds, six foot, six inches tall, whose "secret weapon" was a piece of *"Ivory Soap,"* that he tucked in the belt line of his trunks, and when he placed a "head lock" on opponent, rubbed soap in eyes, causing opponent to stagger blindly all over the ring, referee conveniently looked away, watching spectators, while "Black Jack" twisted his victim's arm as though it were a wet towel. The fans yelling their lungs out until they became bug eyed, pointing at this dastardly deed, questioning referee's eyesight and his inability to catch the obvious infraction, as well as his paternity. The blacks, who filled the balcony to overflowing, bombarded the ring with cups, programs, shoes, anything they could throw, to the point of exhaustion, and becoming white-faced.

What fun! In the closing minutes something spectacular occurred, like using a ringside chair to smash the victim's head, causing blood, or a substitute thereof, similar to catsup, to ooze out of his head. "Who could tell the difference? I sure can't," one of the regulars remarked. All this incredible conduct forcing the referee to stop the melee, declare "no contest," "disqualification," which ever terminology seemed to fit the moment. Then, raise the triumphant one's right arm in the air signifying victory, amid wild applause and obvious approval. Villains were escorted from ring by police, as on more than one occasion, black folk exhibited firearms and screamed taunts, threats and verbal abuse.

Naturally, "Buster," arranged for contestants to come in "Bo's" for lunch, drinks or whatever, meet the citizens.

On a night to remember, "Black Jack," met "Tarzan" White, unrelated, in the main event for the World's Championship, or at least Chatham County Championship, the second son, aged 12, was invited to attend, sit at ringside. Half way through the match, after continuously screaming disapproval of "Jack's" tactics, the villain pointed his finger at the child, shouting, "You're next, pip squeak, I'm gonna' get you!" Moments later, without warning, while "Tarzan" hung unceremoniously over the top rope of the ring, choking, gagging, spitting, while clutching his throat area; "Jack" climbed through the ropes, in the young fellow's direction, who, by that time became physically exhausted as a result of extreme hyper-activity. In one jump, bolted out his seat, running as fast as his legs could carry him, out of the arena, towards the men's room, arriving fifteen seconds too late. What a scene! How embarrassing! "Goodness gracious, I was so scared I couldn't breathe," he was heard later, speaking to "Killer" Rosen, who laughed hard enough to fall down two flights of stairs. Oh, it was funny, you damned near ripped your guts out laughing. It occurs to me that, if you live long enough, there are more people you would like to forget than people you would like to remember. I would like, for instance, to forget "Black Jack."

"Buster," through no fault of his, suffered, when fighters he had advertised, did not appear on the card. Usually fighters that were reasonably well known, drew crowds. Ring Announcer: "Well, ladies and gentlemen, we have a last minute cancellation, our main attraction was forced to cancel, due to unforeseen difficulties, in his place, we are pleased to present to you, "Pretty Boy" Floyd, who is undefeated in Illinois, after over thirty fights!" Boos filtered down from the crowd, as "Pretty" was taking his bows. When he bent over, departing his corner, his boxing trunks ripped down the rear seam exposing "Pretty Boys" fanny. Twenty minutes elapsed before a different pair of trunks, fitting the gladiator were produced, then, the Ring Announcer, who was never at a lost for words, said, "This is his coming out party!" Fight lasted one round, as "Pretty" hit the canvas as a result of one severe punch to the abdomen. "I never saw a guy hit that hard before," Buster commented to his manager; "Pretty" said, "Me neither."

This blessed man, deserved great success, and he attained it, without question he has been and will always be Savannah's Greatest, Most Reliable, Promoter of Entertainment, a gentleman, and a scholar, his name should most definitely be enshrined in the Hall of Fame of Savannah, and the State of Georgia; C. J. "BUSTER" WHITE.

When baseball was "King" in the 1940's and 50's, Savannah was indeed fortunate to have Weldon "Windy" Herrin, do the home games play- by-play, and road games, reconstructed with use of Western Union Ticker, complete with recorded crowd noises. His voice was broadcast throughout "Bo Peep's," providing apt description of occurrences on field. Whenever a hit was made, a "Bonggg" sound indicated amount of bases. A single earned one "Bonggg," a home run, four. That sound will always be a fond memory, and listeners thrilled to hear it. W T O C was the radio station, I think it meant, "Windy Tops Our City." A memorable event was Jake Levy pitch for the *"Savannah Indians."* A frequent customer at "Bo's," he was a short, fat fellow, big around as he was tall, but reliable to pitch at least two innings. A delightful character, was a good draw for the home town Jews. Windy's description was colorful, entertaining.

People wondered why the team was named "Indians?" There weren't any Indians on the team, in fact the last Indian was Tomochichi, and all Savannah people know what happened to him, and where he is buried. Meyer provided a suspect explanation, "Connie Mack told me that he owned them, and that he liked Indians, and he owned a baseball team in Philledelphias, and Philledelphias was named after Indians. (Word spelled like Meyer spoke. Wrong, naturally.) "What did he say?" "Huh?"

Bobby Hornstein, contemplated that good teams are named "Indians," because "Rapid Robert" Feller, was his favorite pitcher, and he pitched for the Cleveland Indians.

Needless to say, the conversations were elevating and illuminating, to say the very least. Some contributors were college graduates, makes you wonder, what they studied, and how they graduated.

CHAPTER THIRTEEN

A few days prior to Thanksgiving, 1947, a real smart fellow came by 19 East Congress, dressed in a blue jacket bearing initials, S. H. S. (Savannah High School,) the time honored, mortal enemy of Benedictine Military School, or "ol' B.C." Much has been written about this rivalry, but to tell you the absolute truth, you had to be there to understand and appreciate it. Dismiss from your mind, anything you might have heard about this day, and travel back in time with major actors, who graced the stage of this real gut wrenching, drama.

Many Cadets will tell you S.H.S. stood for Savannah Horse Stable, or worse. This football game was the centerpiece for citizens for over 50 years, it was finely honed into the damnedest rivalry any body ever new, and it gave definition to the word HATE.

"Bo's" was a favorite place or hangout for Cadets for over ten years. All three of his sons graduated from the private Catholic High school, operated by the priests of the Order of St. Benedict. The story goes that they almost had to "burn the school down," to get his second son out of there. But that's another story.

B. C. was a small school, usually numbering about 200 young men, approximately 98% Catholic, located on Bull Street, and Thirty- fourth Street. S.H.S. was a large, public, co-educational school of 1,200 students, on Washington Avenue. Why they chose Thanksgiving Day to vent spleen and hatred is interesting, to say the least. My guess is that the Pilgrims knew what they were doing, after all they fled England in hatred. So, maybe we came by it naturally or by evolution, or perhaps born to it. Whatever, it was serious, intense.

Folks you might ordinarily speak to fifty weeks of the year, you completely ignored, looked away in disgust, and spit. Travel with somebody, don't go it alone, 'cause you could never tell when a fight would break out, and you would be in it. B.C. stay away from *"Jerry George's,"* SHS keep out of "Bo's." Water and oil don't mix. Wear your colors proudly. Students stood up and were counted, parents lived in anxious anticipation, hoping for the best and, that it get over with fast.

No matter what the season held for these two schools, it didn't matter, T-Day was the "big one." Win that one and you had a great year, no doubt about it. Emotions ran high, parades, bon fires, street brawls, were main events the week preceding the game, culminated by a huge mob, riot, down town at intersection of Bull and Broughton Streets, after the game. Did I say GAME? I meant WAR! It was convenient that "Turkey Day" always fell on Thursday, as celebrants required Friday, Saturday and Sunday to recuperate, sober up and heal.

This fellow was looking for a Cadet named "Horse" Monohan, B.C. star footballer. He and "Horse" had met the night before, wherein a fight erupted over some SHS lass, with lovely yellow hair, big blue eyes, youthful bosom, firm hard body, pug nose, peach- like complexion all the way to her ankles. He thought she was his, she thought "Horse" was "special," and yet with all that in her favor, she simply couldn't say "No" to the dashing, handsome Cadet. Now, "I just want to even the score." Within minutes, "Horse" arrived, without further adieu or discussion, the guy named "Leroy" says, "I been lookin' for your sorry ass, all over town, now, you dirty Son of a

....." Before "Leroy" could get the last word out of his mouth, "Horse" hit him with a right uppercut, flooring poor "Leroy," then, standing over him, taunted him, "That's Mister Son of a Bitch, to you!" Joe McGonigle split his pants laughing, told witnesses, "Horse knocked his dick out of doors!" That blue jacket was bathed in red blood.

1947 was memorable. The Benedictine Cadets football team, all 28 strong, was enduring another horrible year on field, "little man's second son was a senior, captain of the cheer leaders, who led the student body in cheering, supposedly, but had very little to do. That year was distinguished by being defeated by Boys High School, Atlanta, Georgia, 48 – 0; Tech High School, Atlanta, 62 – 0. Both of these schools frequently produced All-Americans, that went on to play college football at Georgia Tech, also in Atlanta. It was not unusual for them to "dress-out" sixty players.

A formidable offense the Cadets had not. Three downs, and kick. Run around right end, run around left end, run into the middle of the line. Coach John Scott was no Knute Rockne.

SHS had beaten BC regularly for years. Cadets decided simply, something must be done to boost morale, which was lower than a fat frogs tail. A meeting of ten seniors led by the second son, and "Dock" Milholin, his best friend, decided to construct a wood coffin, paint it blue and white with big SHS on it, place a stuffed figure dressed in "blue jacket" jersey and pants in it, carry it to a pep rally the night before the game. Done deal.

After appropriate speeches by team members, "Willie" Girardeau, "Tucker" White, "Big Foot" McGrath, "Slick" Lowe; coaches and priests, they planned to spend the night at BMS to guard the coffin because word was received that "blue jacket" "pep squad" intended to steal it, paint it maroon, burn it at Bull and Broughton, after the game. Well, now, that is down right un-friendly. There is an old English expression, "Turn About is Fair Play!" Me thinks Mr. Mills taught us that.

Cadets obtained secret information that "blue jackets" acquired an old carriage used to convey coffins to a cemetery, painted it black with derogatory slogans directed at Cadets, their parentage, and Catholics in general. Intending to pull that thing down town, burn it after the game, possibly including second son.

Well, it just didn't turn out that way, dog-gone-it, as Cadets located that carriage and completely demolished it. Only their efforts to burn the coffin remained

Furious "blue jackets" formed gangs before and after the game. Driving their cars up and down streets, speeding, blaring horns, yelling, screaming, taunting Cadets, as they, dressed in their spotless grays, marched into Grayson Stadium on East Victory Drive, in all their splendor. "Mackeral Snappers," "Kitlics," "Cadets got no fathers," a few choice remarks.

Game was lost, but not as bad as anticipated. Man o' man, that post game celebration down town was immense, over 100 fist fights, which many believe to this day contributed greatly to discontinuing the Thanksgiving Day Game. Amidst fighting and "Hell Raising" the coffin was burned. Blood flowed in the street, but in the final analysis, "Old Fort Irish" emerged victors, winning a large majority of fights. The lucky went to "Bo's," "Joe Gildeas," "Johnny Harris,' unlucky, went home. This singular event still sticks in "Blue Jacket Class of 1947's" craw, even now!

It is right and proper to be written, the Irish in Savannah in those days were not only Catholic, but also decent, honest, hard working, God fearing, spirited, good natured, fun loving and loyal. Comprising all the elements that made America great. Certainly, the "Cream of the Crop." Their names are beautiful, lyrical, and contain the letter "N." A few, Kennedy, Mulherin, Griffin, Doolan, Lanigan, Flanigan, Houlihan, McMillan, McNamara, Bouhan, Ryan, Flynn, Mooney, Sheehan, Keene, Spillane, Halligan, McGinn, Heffernan, Conneff, McCracken. How many times students at Tybee made a list of Irish names that included the letter "N." Maybe the record is one hundred fifty. All hailing from "the olde sod." Many settled in two districts, commonly referred to as "Old Fort Irish," and "Lace Curtain Irish." The boys attended "ol' B.C.", girls, St. Vincent's Academy. Such was the composition that with the Jews, made "Bo Peep's" outstanding.

Funny, as you look back over it, two diverse factions united to become one power in "Port City" politics, controlling for many years "the Imperial State of Chatham," bonding life long friendships. May it always be!

CHAPTER FOURTEEN

Over the years, commencing with the period of
Prohibition (1920-1933) Bo Peep became acquainted with
numerous members of "The Mafia," a secret criminal
organization that has wielded great economic and political
control over large segments of Sicilian society that operates
both criminal and legitimate enterprises in this country.
New York City was the place of origin for organized crime
in the United States. Briefly stated, "The Mafia," is a loose
alliance of small groups of men, bound by kinship, or, a
kinship relationship that is assumed when a man becomes a
member, as well as by the "Mafia" code of "omerta," which
requires absolute obedience to, and silence about "Mafia"
activities. One pet saying is, "Don't do business with
anyone, unless you know their grand mother."

Despite efforts of Italian Fascists to destroy the
organization during World War, II, it survived. When the
Fascists fled as a result of the Allied invasion, the "Mafia"
was the only remaining governing structure, and they
worked closely with U. S. forces. A little known, but true
fact. Politics, do indeed, make strange bedfellows.

With Sicilian immigration of the late 19th century,
"Mafia" began to operate in several large U. S. cities.
During Prohibition it monopolized the trade in bootleg
liquor, controlled loan sharking, gambling, and other illicit
enterprises. The name "Mafia" or the title "Cosa Nostra,"
"our affair," is used to encompass the entire spectrum of
organized crime, and is most frequently quoted by law
enforcement community and public in general. Students,
history 102 is now complete. Thank you very much.

133

As stated earlier, "Bo Peep" met Al "Scar Face" Capone, the reputed head of the "Mafia" family in Chicago, Illinois. That early acquaintance blossomed into numerous business contacts. In 1931, he met Vincent Mangano, who became the head of what was to become, the "Gambino" family in New York. There were five families in the New York City segment of "La Cosa Nostra," "Gambino," "Genovese," "Columbo," "Bonano," and "Luchese." Please note that they are all last names, and that each ends with a vowel. Mangano visited Savannah, on vacation, staying at the Savannah Hotel, on Congress Street, next to "Bo Peep's," several times. He loved the atmosphere and ambience. He was in control of "Gambino" family from 1931 to 1951, which is a very long time for anyone to be in control of a major "family." In 1951, Albert "A.A." Anastasia took over the "Gambino Family," later, in 1953, traveled to Savannah, residing at the General Oglethorpe Hotel on Wilmington Island approximately thirty days. Anastasia ruled until 1957 when he was murdered in a barbershop in New York. He and "Bo" struck up a friendship, which led to the second son's introduction, with the admonition that, "he is graduating from law school at University of Georgia, and is going to be a great lawyer. Don't forget, if you need a lawyer down here, call him." That reference was invaluable, benefiting him throughout his legal career. "A.A." formed "Murder, Inc." According to New York Police records, it was the group that killed an estimated 400 people from 1951 to 1957. In 1955 and 1957 he spent considerable time in Savannah, seeking refuge from the wars. Second son met "A.A." on at least three occasions, and in 1955 presented him with one of his business cards, "Attorney at Law." In 1957, "A.A." visited the last time, just thirty days before he was murdered. New

York Police Department sent three of their top detectives to town to inquire about his interests in this "quaint little town."

Charlie "Lucky" Luciano, a "Genovese family" member, one of the most famous mobsters in history, dropped by "the Port City," on several occasions, average length of stay was three days. He got his nickname "Lucky" after he was assaulted by rivals and left for dead. Unfortunately for the rivals, he survived and ultimately became "the power" in New York City. His control began in 1931, continuing until 1946, when as a result of numerous criminal charges against him, he was deported to Italy, and returned to Sicily. He always spent several hours a day just hanging around, giving "Bo Peep" an opportunity to improve his mathematical prowess. "New York Yankees is my team, they get what they want, I like that." Dressed in the latest fashion, drove "the biggest cars on the road." Question: "Do you know when I am the most uncomfortable, completely unprotected?" "No." "When I'm taking a shower." "Bo" said, "I never thought about it, but, you know, you're right." "When I'm away from home, I keep a man sitting right outside my bathroom door," "Lucky" continued, "Fellow can't be too careful today,...."

It is interesting that "Lucky" was succeeded by one Frank Costello, a close, personal friend and associate. "Big Frank, the boss of bosses," kept the "power" in the "Luciano family." A frequent guest at the *"General Oglethorpe Hotel,"* on Wilmington Island, twelve miles south-east from Savannah, towards Tybee Island. Costello was born January 26, 1891 in Cosenza, Italy, his real name was Francesco Castiglia. In the 1920's engaged in bootlegging, gambling operations, in New York, Florida, Louisiana and three other states. He had a sincere feeling of friendship, in addition sharing some of the same interests. When "Lucky" was deported, Frank gathered business in Las Vegas casinos, and "hobnobbed" with New York socialites, politicians and industry leaders. He was, in fact noted for his influence with politicians, a "fashion plate," and all around "man about town;" appeared in newspapers, magazines with other well known dignitaries.

All of this is a part of the fabric of "the Port City." The weaver throughout was "Bo Peep."

Dinner with Frank Costello. A rare opportunity to meet in an intimate surrounding with one of America's most famous gangsters. Few, if any, "Savannah people" experienced this unique and special occasion. "Man, that was one incredible experience. I ate with every one, from the crown heads in Europe, to the bald heads in America, and I'm here to tell you, Frank was the best!" Those words, by "Bo," are memorable. How so?

Well, let us begin at the beginning. Location was a private cottage in the *"General Oglethorpe Hotel"* complex, overlooking the Wilmington River, about which Johnny Mercer wrote the beautiful song, "Moon River."

Arriving promptly at the designated hour of 6:45 P.M., being invited in by two well dressed men, of Italian extraction, Victor "Looks" Imperio and Anthony Eboli, with the greeting: "You are expected." Ushered into the living room, which was furnished plushy, including television, bar, chess table, dining table with six arm chairs. Perfectly grand seafood buffet on crushed ice, including fresh shrimp, back fin only crab meat flown in from Maryland, oysters, clams and conch. Highlighted by three different "home made" sauces, seven beverages. Entering from the private, master bed room, "the man." Clean shaven, dark complexion, dark hair combed straight back, not a hair out of place, deep, dark brown eyes, that could pierce steel; dressed in a tailor made black, 100% all wool, double breasted suit; white silk, long sleeved shirt, French cuffs with gold links; blue silk tie. As "the boys" say, "Sharp as a tack."

Business like, direct, to the point, non-smiling, but pleasant. Gentlemanly, articulate, spoke in short, clipped sentences with a very obvious "Italian-Yankee Accent." All were seated at a glass top table trimmed in brass. Private service from the hotel chef, and two waiters dressed in tuxedos. Imported French red and white wine, variety of fresh fruit, fresh baked rolls, veal with lemon sauce, "branzino con funghi (sea bass with fresh mushrooms,) imported Italian pasta, and a re-fill of fresh shrimp, crab that slept the previous night in Chesapeake Bay, Maryland. Meal was absolutely, incredibly delicious, something to remember, always. Before partaking of any dish, the host was informed that the food had been prepared in the immediate presence of the two men. Additional precaution was taken as each man tasted the main dishes prior to service.

Speaking in a quiet monotone on several subjects, one quickly understood how and why he was, who and what he was. Continuously and intently studied faces of his two guests. His eyes never left the eyes of the person speaking, or being spoken to. You received the distinct impression that this fellow could not be "fooled or played around with." In other words, "Don't mess with Frank."

Dining approximately one hour, thirty minutes; topped off with fresh strawberry tart, canolis, assorted cheeses, Italian imported biscuits, a bottle of wine from *"House of Rothschild,"* in France, vintage 1925, valued at $900.00 a bottle, a case of which was delivered to the cottage upon arrival.

All of the pleasantries out of the way; time came to "get down to business." "Counselor, it goes without saying, that I have a deep, long lasting appreciation for your father, he assures me that I can deal with you in absolute confidence. I have a highly confidential matter that I want you to handle. Here is the information you will need, and money necessary to complete the transaction." A black leather, locked carrying case was retrieved from the master bed room. "Here is Two Hundred Thousand Dollars. Your fee is in addition thereto." "Gasp."

"Don't you want to count it?"

Pause.

"No, sir, if you say it is here, I know that it is here."

Pause.

"Good. Remember, I demand absolute loyalty."

"Yes, sir."

Walking side by side to the entrance, he carefully repeated, I demand absolute loyalty. There is no substitute."

"Sir, I will live up to the confidence placed in me, I will not betray that confidence. Thank you for the opportunity to be of service." An embrace, hand shake, "good bye."

Father and son drove back to Savannah without speaking. Separating, Father said, with tear-filled eyes, "I am so proud of you." "I have a great teacher. You!" Long hug, both men crying. "Good."

On the night of May 2, 1957, Costello was shot in his hotel lobby, allegedly by Vincente "Chin" Gigante, a Vito Genovese gunman, but survived that near death experience. Genovese was Costello's major rival for supremacy in New York's crime cartel. Costello was most frequently referred to as "King of the Slots," as well as "Prime Minister of the Underworld," because of all the cops and politicians he "owned."

He died of a heart attack on February 18, 1973 in New York.

His funeral was one of the largest in New York City history, attended by Frank Sinatra, numerous movie stars, celebrities and politicians. Over two hundred car procession, was provided an "official" thirty N. Y. P. D. motor cycle police escort. Burial site was filled to capacity. Buried in a large crypt in St. Michael's Cemetery Astoria, Queens County, New York, after a high mass conducted by a Bishop.

Sadly, it was reported in the *New York Times,* that someone later broke into his crypt, disturbing the corpse, while looking for jewelry.

CHAPTER FIFTEEN

ST. PATRICK'S DAY IN SAVANNAH IS AN
EXPERIENCE UNLIKE ANY OTHER. IT IS THE
ONLY PLACE ON THE PLANET TO BE WHEN
MARCH 17th ROLLS AROUND!

Nobody knew that better than "Bo." Special
decorations adorned his 154 feet fronting on Congress
Street; Irish flags, Orange, Green and White bunting and
welcome signs. A special menu of Corned Beef, shipped in
from Chicago, Illinois, and Cabbage fresh from the City
Market, together with all brands of beer known to man.
"What'll you have, *Pabst Blue Ribbon?*" "Any time is
Miller's time!" Employees participated in the theme,
dressed in green or wore green ties with imported
shamrocks. "Happy St. Pat's Day," and "Erin Go Bragh,"
punctuated greetings and well wishes. Sure, faith and
begorrah, everybody was Irish on that day. Even Epstein!

The Day begins with a Mass at Cathedral of St. John
the Baptist, on Abercorn Street, followed by the "World's
Biggest Parade!" However, an integral part of that
spectacular, prior to parading, marchers filed in for "a little
beer" or "tonic." Story goes that on one celebration, the
aroma of alcohol permeated the church's atmosphere so
severely that, priest had to pause in the proceedings, and
request that communicants keep their heads bowed, thus
preventing priestly intoxication.

Sixty year old, "Coxie" Brind was always early,
anxious to get a head start, dressed in green jacket, yellow
pants, green tie, shamrock in lapel, Irish flag in hand; red
face and nose, telling anyone that listened, "It's Great to be

140

Irish, don't you forget that!" "Hi ya!" "It's great to be Irish! Don't you forget that!"

Juke Box, appropriately loaded with Irish songs, played constantly, a piano "player" hired for the occasion, belted forth "When Irish Eyes are Smiling," McNamara's Band," "Dear Old Donegal," and "That's an Irish Lullaby," from dawn to mid-night. "Too-ra-loo-ra-loo-ra, That's an Irish Lullaby!"

"Good Golly, Miss Molly, what a scene to behold."

A perfectly happy, fun, place to be. No admission charge, ever, although numerous celebrants reported, "Hell, this is worth Twenty Dollars to be here!"

The Parade has a legendary history all its own, anyone born and raised in Savannah has at least one story to tell about it. Of course, The Benedictine "Marching Band," all thirty-six of them, led, playing their hearts out. They knew three different tunes, played them over and over. "B. C. Fight Song," "McNamara's Band," one, which name, couldn't remember. Entire Cadet Corps all dressed out in "Dress Grays," white pants, white cross belts, hat covers; black, "spit shined" shoes sparkling in the sun. A thing of beauty and a joy forever. Parade route packed with proud Mothers, with tear filled eyes, watching their sons strut their stuff. "Hey Margaret, there's my son, Harold!" "I know it, how he's grown!" "Please, get a picture if you can."

Arriving at the intersection of Bull and Broughton Streets, the roar of the crowd was deafening. Confetti, paper ribbons, balloons, filled the air. There is absolutely, positively nothing like it anywhere! Parade ended in Troup Square, a few blocks from "Bo's," so naturally the boys had to come back, for some rest, relaxation. "Thank you!"

CONCLUSION

Things were changing in Savannah in 1951. New political alliances were being formed that did not include "Bo Peep." The young and restless created a "party" named auspiciously enough, "Citizens Progressive League."

What a joke, those guys wouldn't know progress if it bit them on their collective legs. The town had not progressed in one hundred years, nevertheless, they wanted their chance. Although they spoke about "improving" Savannah, they had for the most part, lived their lives there, and could not point to one "improvement" at their hands.

"C. P. L.'s" sole objective, beat long time, entrenched political machine, master-minded by one John J, Bouhan, who for many years, "ran the county," as County Attorney.

Two weeks prior to *"The Savannah Morning News"* publishing a back page story that the "old line" was to be opposed, two of the so- called "leaders" of the "League" visited "Bo Peep."

First of which was an Irish-Catholic lawyer, with a big head, shoulders and stomach, who looked as though he'd burst into song, "When Irish Eyes are Smiling." He maintained an office within three blocks of "Bo's" and was a customer for some years. "Hale fellow, well met type," trying to establish a reputation as a criminal trial and divorce lawyer. Consequently he solicited business from "Bo," and, on occasion, placed $20.00 bets on football and baseball games. He possessed a hearty appetite, "booze head, whore hopper," earned distinction of having sex with female clients, instead of customary monetary consideration; which, of course was highly unethical.

142

Clearly, it was a memorable Friday afternoon, lawyer "Jack" O'Brien dropped in to "chat for a while." Inclement weather was a good excuse, after usual "glad handing, good to see ya'" stuff was over, he got right down to business.

"Bo, you know, we have been friends for years, and, I like you. I'm one of the individuals forming a new political party for the city elections, want you to know, that you will always have a friend in me. We're opening our campaign office in two weeks, several of the fellows, you already know, but you will need someone on the inside, to make certain you're protected, and, business continue as usual."

Warming to the task, "Jack" sipped on a gin and tonic, rubbed his hands together as if cold; straightened blue and gold stripped neck tie, buttoned jacket, cleared throat, with smile on his face, continued, "I'll make you a deal, send me $500.00 per week, in cash, to my office Friday of each week, and I'll personally guarantee that you can keep on doing business as usual."

"Bo," by this time was sipping a glass of cold water, removed eye glasses, looked "Jack" squarely in the eyes, saying, "I'll think about it. Hold on a minute, I'll get you a check now for $500.00 to help the League with opening expenses. Give me a week to consider this, come back to see me. Thanks, I appreciate your consideration." "Jack" swallowed the beverage, folded the check, said, "That's one helluvah deal for you, can't beat it, and you thought we'd be hard to work with...this way, we'll all be happy."

Who woulda thunk it?

Next day, Saturday, a surprise visitor came to see "Mr. Bo." Introduced himself to "Tiger," and second son, was escorted to the lunch counter for a brief wait.

This fellow also was a lawyer, Christ Church member, medium build, resembled a mole in the face, wore white

143

shirt, red tie and seer- sucker suit, or what the "boys" called, "mattress covers." In fact, this fellow looked exactly like what we all knew as W. A. S. P., white, Anglo-Saxon, protestant. Certainly, he had no time for blacks or other minorities, including Jews, was a name member of a small law firm, specializing in everything, offices within three blocks of 19 East Congress Street. The type that wouldn't be "caught dead in Bo Peep's."

"Hey, Mister Silver, I should have called for appointment to see you, but I figured you'd be here. My name is Orville Bragg, my friends call me O. B. I guess you've heard by now that the C. C. D. C., or whatever they're called, is going to have serious opposition in the up-coming election."

Without pausing, he pressed on, "I'm one of the small group comprising leadership, in fact, I spearheaded it for the past year along with some Jaycees. You might call me, a founding father, and I will be in on all political decisions and patronage. I feel reasonably certain, that you want to remain in business, doing whatever it is that you do, and I will help you, this, of course, being a two-way street, you know, you scratch my back, I'll scratch yours. What I need is Five Hundred Dollars per week, cash money, delivered to my office on Friday of each week, beginning Friday after our election. For that, I'll guarantee you'll be alright, all I need is an O.K. and hand shake."

"Sir, I thank you, let me think this over, I'll call you next week… if that's O.K. with you. Nice to see you, Bye."

"Good Lord, in all my years here, I've never seen anything like that fellow and the other one who was in here earlier," carefully relaying the conversations to "Tiger." "Arrogant, greedy, S. O. B's, never in my life have I received propositions like that, it is entirely unreasonable, they must think I'm printing money over here. I've already talked with Mister Myrick and Mister Bouhan, they both expressed amazement, besides, they think the C. C. D. C. will survive, so,... I guess my mind's made up, ...no deal."

Five days later, "Jack" came in, double parking his shiny new *Cadillac* convertible out front on Congress Street, exhibiting a pretty young thing in the front seat. "Bo, I'm in a big hurry," demonstrating that smiling, happy face. "We got a deal?"

"No, Jack, I cannot go along with your deal, there's no way I can make that nut, sorry, I have to pass..."

Suddenly that smile turned into a frown, removing his tie, Jack stated, "Alright, remember, if we win, you lose."

They did and he did.

You might call that a bit of bad luck, or bad business decision.

After a series of bad decisions, not only by "the little man," but also by his family, the property was sold, business closed in 1955. Three people attempted to open businesses based upon his model, however, they were all doomed to fail.

The heart of Savannah had stopped beating.

It is common knowledge, a body cannot survive if the heart stops beating. Savannah was about to learn that important maxim. A once vibrant, thriving, busy "downtown" began to deteriorate to the point that it became a ghost town. "Broughton became Broughtoff." Almost all of the main businesses closed, "Bo Peep's," Bijou Theatre, Fine's Ladies Apparel, Style Shop, Morris Levy's, Adler's Department Store; B. H. Levy's Department Store. Without exception the store owner, clerks and employees of each were regular customers of "Bo's." Paradise lost,

145

gave rise to a frequent complaint, "What's a fellow got to do during lunch time?" "Yes, sir, this was the "progress" carefully planned by the C. P. L."

Troubles that mounted up over the previous two years, took heavy toll, too burdensome, even for a super man. The bar, open for over twenty-five years, suddenly became "too close to Christ Church." "Change, or close." Uniformed police began to show up, stand around, look for any thing "out of the ordinary." Sanitation Department searched for violations, and found only a need for a double sink. "Change or close, take your choice." "Fix it, now!"

Early in 1955, he consulted with several of the town's most enterprising real estate brokers, including Bernard B. Eichholz, T. J. Mc Ginley, William H. "Bill" Lynes. Each was anxious to "list" the property for sale, in fact, two of them begged for it.

It did not take long, purchasers were arranged, and dreams of over twenty-six years came to an abrupt halt. Architectural drawings by one of Atlanta's prominent architects to erect a ten story hotel on corner of his property, to bear the name of Franklin D. Roosevelt, was abandoned.

As news leaked out, close friends and employees could not believe it, - "No way, little man will save the day." But, it was not to be. Words will not express the feelings of great personal loss, humiliation and embarrassment that tiny little man felt, he simply did not nor could not realize what had happened to him on the way to the culmination of his life's dream.

On that final, gray day, when "Bo Peep's Billiard Parlor" ceased to do business, it rained "cats and dogs." A. L. Karp, his C. P. A. observed, "Even the angels in heaven are crying."

Turning the keys over to the broker, he shook hands all around, saving the nearest and dearest for the last, and quietly started to leave by way of the front door, when Morris Levy, owner of the men's store bearing his name, neighbor for over twenty years, approached, embraced the little man warmly, "I'll tell you one thing Wolfie, I will miss you so very much, this town won't ever be the same. I love you." Both men wept openly, un-ashamed. "Morris, you have been great to me and my family, take care, and, I love you, too."

"Clayton," the doorman for over twenty years at the adjacent *Savannah Hotel,"* proceeded hesitantly, rain drops running down his moon shaped face and red, full length rain coat. Slowly removing his white gloves, wiped his face with back of his hand, cleared his throat with an "Ahem," stated, "God knows I'm gonna' miss you something awful, Congress Street won't be the same without you, this damn town won't. If there's anything I can do, any time, please call me." Then automatically, "Mr. Bo, do you need a cab?"

"No, Clayton, thank you, I want you to know that I appreciate every thing you did for me, all these years..." Choking up, he was unable to complete the sentence. "Thank you, old friend."

The last farewell, appropriately enough, was "Johnny" Ware, who was obviously uncomfortable and ill at ease. Through tight lips, straining to be heard, blurted out, "...please take care,...."

By this time, the little man began to weep. Choking, he pulled a white handkerchief from his right hand back pocket, dabbed his eyes, wiped his glasses, slowly, almost haltingly, began that walk he had made a million times previously to the front door, for the final time. His head dropped slowly as though he was nodding, shoulders sagged, after taking ten strides, inhaled deeply, squared his little frame, looked heavenward, murmuring to himself, "Please God, have mercy on my soul."

With that, the double glass front doors opened simultaneously, the "little man" exited without looking back, mercifully missing that there was not a dry eye in the crowd of fifteen spectators.

"Good bye, Mister Bo Peep, good bye."

He met the second son, they walked together, without speaking toward a waiting vehicle. As they passed through Johnson Square, rain abated, a group of four young black men were softly singing,

"Oh they say some people long ago
Were searching for a different tune,
One that they could croon as only they can."
(Birth of The Blues, by Lew Brown/B.G. DeSylva/Ray Henderson.)
"How appropriate...don't you think?"
Silence prevailed.

DEATH.

How does one write of death, when

1. It is a loved one;
2. A parent;
3. Best friend, teacher;
4. Benefactor, personal hero?

Not easily.

"Bo Peep's" death came suddenly, completely without warning, shockingly, in middle of night. In good health, he had returned to Savannah two days earlier, to be with his second son, registered as a guest in *The John Wesley Hotel*, on Congress Street, diagonally across from his former business location.

On July 7, 1963 at approximately 7:45 P.M., second son had a fifteen minute telephone conversation with him, he talked in firm tone of "tomorrow," without stress, regular, routine matters. That was the final conversation anyone had with him. His last words were, "That's good enough for me."

Early morning, following day, second son left town on a 'business trip to Statesboro, Georgia. At 3:45 P.M., stopped at a Pure Oil Service Station to fill up for return trip.

Approaching the station, after pumping gas, he observed a *Savannah Evening Press* newspaper stand, and, for the shock of his life, observed on the front page thereof, a photograph of his Father, and a column announcing his death.

That moment of that day was the most excruciating, profoundly distressing, painful event, ever in his life. Nothing before, or after, could even closely approximate such grief, regret, sorrow and despair. Severely engraving in his memory, permanent, indelible impression.

Struggled with that awful reality all the way home; fervently attempted to summon up courage, find some expression to settle his aching, tormented heart and mind. "God's finger touched him and he slept."

Immediately upon arriving home, he was greeted by his wife and two young children, informed that it was he, who had to make arrangements, identify the body. Proceed without delay to *Sipple's Mortuary* on Abercorn Street, to perform the most unpleasant of human tasks.

149

"My God!"

From that day until this, not one day has passed without thought of his Father. Often remarked, if he had one day to re-live, it was July 7, 1963. Time stood still, the day his Father died. Oh, how he would have liked to see him just one more time, say "Good bye," express how much he meant to him, how much he loved him. Day after day he thought, "I miss you a little, few old memories keep hanging on, I miss you a little too much, a little too often, a little more every day. I drive by our old house, pretend you are still there waiting for me, on the side porch, but all I see is an empty chair. I wish I could see you one more time before I drive away." Each succeeding day, and on every personal success, he always says, "I wish my Father was here to see this." Some argue that he is!

"Death is a fearful thing," Shakespeare wrote in *"Measure for Measure."* Second son will testify to that.

Certificate of Death indicated, "death by strangulation." Suggesting it was by his own hand, although that conclusion has been challenged by people who knew him well. Perhaps, perhaps not; we will never know for sure. Stranger things than that have happened in "the land of milk and honey, and the city of good and evil." One thing is certain, notion of people contemplating suicide, talk about it, give verbal warnings, is completely destroyed here. There was none of that. No "I'm tired, I'm sick, I can't go on."

People closest to him felt then and feel now, that he died of a "broken heart." There is ample proof that people he helped most, turned their backs on him, without exception, "like rats off a sinking ship." Of the countless legions that he rendered aid, assistance, support, both moral and financial, not one made slightest effort to help him, not one. Not one found one minute of time to talk, or show the least bit of consideration, or extend an act of kindness. The bridge over which so many trod to their own success, was closed to the bridge keeper. That says a great deal about Savannah, says it all.

Too bad, Savannah!

Henry Wadsworth Longfellow wrote:

"Tell me not, in mournful numbers,
Life is but an empty dream!
For the soul is dead that slumbers,
And things are not what they seem.

Life is real! Life is earnest!
And the grave is not its goal;
Dust thou art, to dust returnest,
Was not spoken of the soul.

Lives of great men all remind us
We can make our lives sublime,
And, departing, leave behind us
Footprints on the sands of time."

Wolfe William "Bo Peep" Silver, left his foot prints on the sands of time.

He will always be remembered as one who made the world a better place than when he entered.

Loyal to his friends and family.

He loved his God.

He loved America.

He loved his family, and tried with his last ounce of courage, to reach the un-reachable stars.

Inscribed upon his tombstone are the words, "AT REST."

May he Rest In Peace.

And, oh yes, may the peace of the Lord be with him always.

"THIS BO PEEP AIN'T NO FAIRY TALE!"

SAVANNAH, REVISITED.

Shortly after the hoopla about Millennium 2000 subsided, second son returned to Savannah for a brief visit. Weather is the same, parks still beautiful, old Victorian style architecture attractive, Bonaventure Cemetary, all, the way he recalled it. Dinner at *Johnny Harris' Restaurant,* drive to Tybee, visit to Drayton and Congress Streets intersection. About 7:00 P.M., darkness began to descend, the street light casting an eerie pall. Enough to make your skin crawl.

Three men were talking so loud, it was easy to hear what was being said. Suddenly one exclaimed, "Oh, My God, there he is; I'm sure that's him, I'd know that walk anywhere, that's him, that's the little man, that's Bo Peep. So help me God, there he is!"

"Where, I don't see him, that's not him, you must have had too much *Johnny Walker Black* to drink!"

"Nah, Hell no, that's him, here he comes,…Hey Bo, is that you?"

"I'm telling you that ain't him, he passed away years ago, I went to his funeral, Sipple Mortuary handled details, … you know, I was born sixty-nine years ago, I used to go to his place just about every afternoon with Captain "Buck" Moran of the City Fire Department; we'd spend hours there after work, just talking, shootin' the breeze, there was always something goin' on, someone to talk with take a sip or two, maybe a cold brew, just have a good time. When he closed, that all went with him, today's old timers got nowhere to go, nothin' to do, except sit at some bar and dream of what might have been ...ain't it funny how time slips away?"

"Yeah, I remember Captain Louie Miller, he too, was a fireman, he could talk the ears off a brass monkey, had a lot to say 'bout ev'ry little thing and ev'ry body, thought he could shoot pool..., but I took him easily. He's the only guy I ever knew that took thirty minutes to drink one cup of coffee, I honestly believe he read the print off the newspaper."

"What a man, but, hey, don't get him mad...he was all man!"

"Remember old Joe Kent, the rubber man, personal service, curb service, an authentic character...used to carry them things around in a nice wood box, display them like precious jewels, what a guy!"

"Yeah, man, you are goin' back, now you testin' my mem'ry... how about Tommy "Black Tom" Thomas, he was really somethin' else, had a most serious, intense expression I ever saw, talked so damn fast, I couldn't keep up...then "Hank" Wiseman, "Boogie" Blair, son of H. Blair, the tailor, had a shop across Drayton, here, for thirty years, came in "Bo's" ev'ry day, at least once; "Salt" Owens, a merchant seaman; Julius Fine a lawyer; Billy Searcey, another lawyer."

"That was the place to be, nothin' like it now or ever; you know, they tore down paradise to make it a parking lot!"

"Ho, ho, ho, you got that right, that's Savannah for you, I'll tell you somethin' else, there ain't nothin' but the dead

and dying in my home town! Paul Simon and Art
Garfunkel had it exactly right."

"Well, I got to be moseying along, nice to see you
again, and hey, if you got nothin' to do, drop by *Mc
Donald's* tomorrow, have breakfast, cold eggs, greasy
potatoes, pure dreck! Maybe some old guys will be there."

"That reminds me, coffee, remember how good that
coffee was in that thick polished ceramic cup, that kept it
hot, not that Styrofoam crap; I asked "Bo" once, what was
the secret ingredient made it tasty, he said, one pad of
butter in ten gallons...I can taste it now! "Big" Elliott
Gottlieb brought in those delicious cinnamon twist rolls,
fresh from his bakery ev'ry morning, and the pies and rolls
were superb. What ever happened to *Gottleib's Bakery?"*

"Who the Hell knows!"

"See you, Ace!"

"You too, Shorty!"

"Thanks for the memories."

Second son took a deep breath, it was darker now, as he
watched the men walk slowly away, their conversation
ringing in his ears. Quickly glancing around, there wasn't a
bench to sit on, just an empty parking lot. He shuddered as
he thought, wow, what he would give to have that one final
meeting. That is the stuff that dreams are made of, that is
for the movie makers.

Moving snail like, he had to look over his left shoulder,
one more time in the direction from whence that figure
emerged; can you top that, he mused, "I can't believe it,
and I saw it with my own eyes!"

Following three days he was restless, irritable and
extremely ill at ease...with an impatience that he could not
explain.

"It is true that he still dominates that intersection...even now!"

About the Author

Murray M. Silver was born in Savannah, Georgia on October 15, 1929, the second son of Wolfe W. Silver and Catherine M. Silver. He attended Charles Ellis Elementary School, Richard Arnold Junior High School, and Benedictine Military School, graduating in the class of 1947. Then he graduated from Armstrong Junior College in 1949, and entered the University of Georgia Law School in September of that year. His studies were interrupted when he was called to active duty in the United States Air Force during the Korean War. He graduated from Law School in 1953, and was admitted to the practice of law in October, 1953, entering private practice, with offices in the Savannah Bank and Trust Building overlooking Johnson Square.

He was President of class of 1947 alumni; Chancellor of Tau Epsilon Phi Fraternity at the University of Georgia; President of B'nai B'rith; Manager and Coach of a Little League Baseball team three years, winning the city championship twice. Named to "Who's Who in American Law, 1978." Member of the Georgia Bar for 44 years; admitted to practice in the United States Supreme Court, Court of Appeals; and numerous District Courts. A prominent trial lawyer, handling over 3,000 cases in 42 states, the District of Columbia and Argentina, England, Bahamas, Jamaica and Antigua. His clients came from all walks of life, including William B. Shockley, Nobel Laureate; five "Godfathers;" and "The World's Biggest Drug Trafficker."

He was appointed General Counsel of the Georgia Department of Labor, by Hon. S. Sam Caldwell, serving three years before returning to private practice in Atlanta, Ga. Memberof the Board of Advisors of the Martin Luther King, Jr., Center for Non-Violent Social Change, Coretta Scott King, President. Appointed Judge of Municipal Court of Atlanta, Ga., by Hon. Andrew Young, Mayor; a Mason. Member of Scottish Rite and YAARAB Temple.

Married to the former Barbara Ann Kahn, Savannah, two sons, Murray M. Silver, Jr., and Eric C. Silver.

Printed in the United States
2510